A Teacher's Choice Award Winner!

"Handy, quick, thought provoking, and age appropriate. A great book filled with sequential, easy-to-handle topics and lesson plans that don't take up a lot of time."
—*Learning* Magazine

Quick and Lively Classroom Activities

Meaningful Ways to Keep Kids Engaged During Transition Time, Downtime, or Anytime

By Linda Nason McElherne, M.A.

Illustrated by Ken Vinton
Edited by Marjorie Lisovskis

free spirit
PUBLiSHiNG®

Helping kids
help themselves™
since 1983

Library of Congress Cataloging-in-Publication Data
McElherne, Linda Nason, 1953–
    Quick and lively classroom activities : meaningful ways to keep kids engaged during transition time, downtime, or anytime / by Linda Nason McElherne ; illustrated by Ken Vinton ; edited by Marjorie Lisovskis.
        p.   cm.
        Includes index.
        Rev. ed. of: Jump-starters. 1999.
        ISBN-13: 978-1-57542-214-5
        ISBN-10: 1-57542-214-X
1. School children—Psychology. 2. Self-esteem—Study and teaching (Elementary) 3. Cooperativeness—Study and teaching (Elementary) 4. Creative activities and seat work. I. Lisovskis, Marjorie. II. McElherne, Linda Nason, 1953– Jump-starters. III. Title.

    LB1117.M334 2006
    372.13—dc22   2006006994

At the time of this book's publication, all facts and figures cited are the most current available. All telephone numbers, addresses, and Web site URLs are accurate and active; all publications, organizations, Web sites, and other resources exist as described in this book; and all have been verified as of February 2006. The author and Free Spirit Publishing make no warranty or guarantee concerning the information and materials given out by organizations or content found at Web sites, and we are not responsible for any changes that occur after this book's publication. If you find an error or believe that a resource listed here is not as described, please contact Free Spirit Publishing. Parents, teachers, and other adults: We strongly urge you to monitor children's use of the Internet.

The semaphore alphabet on page 22 and the hieroglyphic alphabet on page 154 are adapted from *Alphabet Antics: Hundreds of Activities to Challenge and Enrich Letter Learners of All Ages* by Ken Vinton (Minneapolis: Free Spirit Publishing, 1996) and are used with permission of the publisher.

Some of the activities in this book are adapted from or include ideas from contributions made by author and editor Pamela Espeland ("Who Am I?") and teachers Delana Heidrich ("My Greatest Hope," "What I Want My Teacher to Know," and "Taking Care of Myself"), Ruth Rosenberg ("Getting to Know You"), and Susan Luppino ("Learning New Words").

Author photograph by Jay C. Shadowens
10 9 8 7 6 5 4 3 2 1
Printed in the United States of America

Free Spirit Publishing Inc.
217 Fifth Avenue North, Suite 200
Minneapolis, MN 55401-1299
(612) 338-2068
help4kids@freespirit.com
www.freespirit.com

As a member of the Green Press Initiative, Free Spirit Publishing is committed to the three Rs: Reduce, Reuse, Recycle. Whenever possible, we print our books on recycled paper containing a minimum of 30% post-consumer waste. At Free Spirit it's our goal to nurture not only children, but nature too!

green press INITIATIVE

Dedication

With love, I dedicate this to Angela Anne, my mother,
who figuratively stood by me and gave of her time.

And to Katherine Lynn, my little daughter,
who literally stood by me and tried to be part of the writing experience.

Acknowledgments

With deep appreciation, I would like to thank my family, teachers, principals, librarians, and friends, as well as Free Spirit, for helping me accomplish my goal. This book is a combined effort. Though my name appears on the title page, I could not have written the book without the collaborative effort of many others.

My heartfelt thanks go:

To James, Elizabeth, Robert, and Katherine, my children, who inspire me, fill my head with ideas, and add humor to a long day. To Angela and Pete Nason, my parents, who promote education.

To Pamela Espeland, Delana Heidrich, Ruth Rosenberg, and Susan Luppino for their ideas and contributions that are woven into the material presented on these pages.

To the students of Monroe School who bring their minds, hearts, and creativity to the programs that I develop and teach. Because of their eagerness and willingness to experiment with new concepts, they enhance my creativity.

To numerous libraries, especially the Hinsdale Public Library, where dedicated and diligent librarians and resource people helped me track down the materials and information that I needed to strengthen the content of this book. And I cannot neglect to give special thanks to all of the authors whose books and other resource materials inspired me.

Special thanks to Margie Lisovskis, the editor of this book, and to Judy Galbraith and Elizabeth Verdick at Free Spirit Publishing for their guidance, support, and insight throughout the creation of *Quick and Lively Classroom Activities*.

Contents

List of Reproducible Pages

Introduction

"The human mind, once stretched to a new idea, never goes back to its original dimensions."
Oliver Wendell Holmes (1809–1894), U.S. author and physician

Jump right into *Quick and Lively Classroom Activities!* This book will help you fill fifteen- to twenty-minute periods during the school day—those early morning, late afternoon, or "between" times—with meaningful activities your students will enjoy. You will find literally *hundreds* of simple, stimulating ways to build self-esteem, promote creativity, develop cooperation, and make learning fun.

The enrichment activities in *Quick and Lively Classroom Activities* can be linked not only to self-help, but also to language arts, science, geography, social studies, and the arts. They broaden kids' horizons by inviting them to walk new avenues of life, try new things, explore new ideas, and make new discoveries. Your students will come away with a better understanding and appreciation of themselves and others, and a greater appreciation of the wonderful experiences they can have in your classroom.

What's in This Book?

Quick and Lively Classroom Activities is a collection of projects and discussion topics for grades 3–6. They are interesting for students and easy for teachers to implement. Whether you use them at the beginning, middle, or end of the day, during homeroom time or the midday blahs, you'll find they can "jump start" your classroom by involving young learners in exploring goals and dreams, improving personal relationships, being creative, and building skills for success in school and in life.

The activities are arranged in five broad sets: "Knowing Myself," "Getting to Know Others," "Succeeding in School," "Life Skills," and "Just for Fun." Grouped within the five sets are fifty-two themes—one for each week of the year, although they are *not* linked to the calendar and you can use them in any order you choose. Each theme offers five activities—a full week's worth—for a total of 260 activities in all.

What's in a Theme?

You'll find a variety of themes, including "A Walk in Your Shoes," "Managing My Time," "What I Want My Teacher to Know," "Setting Goals," "Taking Care of Myself," "Showing My Art and Soul," and "What's Important to Me?" Each theme includes the following elements:

Quotation

An introductory quotation sets the stage for the theme's activities. You might want to read it aloud to your students.

Introduction

A brief introduction explains the purpose or rationale for the activities. It's written so you can read it aloud to your students, if you like.

Five Activities

Every activity is designed to be completed within fifteen to twenty minutes. In most cases, the activities can stand alone and can therefore be completed in any sequence. This means you may choose themes and activities based on your needs for a particular day. In some cases, some or all of a theme's activities follow a sequence. A note at the beginning of the theme alerts you to this.

The activities are written in kid-friendly language so you can simply read the instructions out loud, if you wish. This approach may be comfortable and convenient for you, or you may prefer to describe the activities in your own words.

The activities employ five different learning styles or modalities. Symbols identify these modalities:

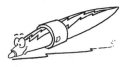 **Writing activities** invite students to compose autobiographies, essays, poems, songs, short stories, lists, ads, flyers, and letters.

 **Drawing activities** take students into the world of cartoons, calligraphy, cityscapes, still lifes, landscapes, murals, and posters.

 **Creative activities** involve students in creating or exploring collages, music, skits, sculpture, experiments, puzzles, or charts.

 **Music and movement activities** let students get physical as they dance, play games, stretch, walk, role-play, exercise, and pantomime.

 **Activities with an emphasis on reaching out to others** offer students the opportunity to participate in service actions for someone else, for their school, or for their community.

Some activities include reproducible handouts, which you'll find immediately following the individual themes. For a list of reproducible pages, see page v.

Theme Builders

 Think about it, talk about it discussion starters help summarize or extend the ideas explored in the activities.

 An **affirmation** closes each theme with words of support and encouragement to reinforce the message or skill students have explored.

 **Resources** at the end of each theme relate to some or all of the activities.

Most of the resources are appropriate for students to use directly; a few, noted "For Teachers," offer information that will be more useful to the teacher or other adult overseeing the activities. You will find these resources particularly helpful if you wish to further develop an activity or theme.

How to Use This Book

You can randomly select a different activity each day or choose from themes that are designed for a longer two- to five-day involvement. If you find a theme or activity you'd like to extend, use your own creativity along with the suggested resources to expand the theme.

The materials required for most of the activities are common school supplies. When an activity calls for a few extra materials, they are easily obtainable.

No activity has a right or wrong interpretation. Each should be evaluated, if at all, on the student's individual participation and group interaction.

Write to Me

I would love to hear how *Quick and Lively Classroom Activities* works for you. Please write to me c/o Free Spirit Publishing, 217 Fifth Avenue North, Suite 200, Minneapolis, MN 55401-1299, or email help4kids@freespirit.com.

I hope you enjoy sharing the book with your students as much as I have enjoyed writing it.

Linda Nason McElherne
Hinsdale, Illinois

Knowing Myself

Who Am I?

"I think self-awareness is probably the most important thing towards being a champion."

Billie Jean King, U.S. tennis champion

The more you know about yourself, the more you can use your talents, skills, and abilities to reach your potential. Self-awareness is the key that unlocks the door to liking and knowing yourself better. Show who you are!

Name Collage

drawing paper • magazines • scissors • glue • markers

Show how your name fits you. Create a collage or a group of letters and symbols that illustrates who you are. Cut pictures and words from magazines or draw a picture of your name with images and letters. Illustrate your first name, last name, or both. Look at your picture-name. Do you think it suits you? Do others think so?

Lollipop Self-Portrait

bubble gum • lollipops in wrappers • colored paper • scissors • glue

Tip: If you can't use gum, a little clay or Play-Doh works just as well.

Be a 3-D "portrait pop"—a lollipop fashioned to look like *you*. While you spend a minute chewing gum, think about how you will show a portrait of yourself using a lollipop and colored paper. Put the softened gum on a piece of paper. Insert the lollipop stick in the gum base. The wrapped candy top will be your head. The stick will be your skeleton. Cut small pieces of paper to create your facial features, hair, and clothes. Glue them on. Add details that make the sculpture uniquely you. Enjoy this artful treat after you complete it.

Favorite Snack

Compare yourself to your favorite treat. Is your personality like *granola*—a mix of interesting and very different qualities? Do you bubble and fizz like *soda*? Are you bright, perky, and *apple-cheeked*? Long, lean, and lanky like *licorice*? Discuss these ideas in small groups. Do others see the same connections?

Favorite Music

radio or CD or tape player with favorite music

All together now, lip-sync and mime to music you enjoy. Let it bring out your fun and physical side. Dance, sing, and move alone or in small groups, just like the masterful musicians of your time. Why do you like these entertainers? How do their words and music speak to you? About you?

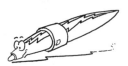

Guess Who?

small slips of paper (fortune-cookie size) • small film canisters (free at photo shops)

Jot down facts and memories about your life—information that would help someone know it's you. Were you part of a school game, play, or concert? Are you famous for your sense of humor? Write your clues on small slips of paper. Place them in a film container. Mix up the containers and pick one out. Read someone else's clues. Can you guess who it is?

Think About It, Talk About It

- You are about to be introduced to a great world leader (a president, king or queen, or prime minister). She or he wants to know who you are—but you can only say one sentence. What will you say?

- Why is it important to know who you are?

- Is it possible to be too self-aware? Why or why not?

Affirmation

I'll get to know myself better.

Resources

For Students

Charlip, Remy, Lillian Moore, and Vera B. Williams. *Hooray for Me!* (Tricycle Press, 1996). This cheery celebration of self by a trio of award-winning picture book creators provides delightful food for thought ("I am my shadow's body," "I am my cousin's cousin"). Ages 4–8.

Stein, Deborah. *Attitude in a Jar™ for Kids* (Honor Press, 1995). Inside this jar are 365 attitude slips designed to help young people feel good about themselves and face each day with insight. All ages.

Celebrating Myself

**"Never bend your head. Always hold it high.
Look the world straight in the eye."**

Helen Keller (1880–1968), U.S. writer and educator

It's important to know what you value in yourself. Like breakfast cereal that fuels your body, your strengths, talents, and unique qualities energize your mind and spirit. Promote yourself!

Note: Do the "Celebrating Myself" activities in sequence.

Cereal-Box Self

clean, empty cereal boxes • copies of handout on page 8

Bring in an empty cereal box—make sure the sides, bottom, and top aren't torn. Get into a group and look at your cereal boxes together. What catches your eye? What keeps you interested? Make a plan to be a cereal-box celebrity. Think about how you can "package" yourself on your box. Look at the handout for some ideas. Will you use a photo that you're proud of? Will you draw yourself? Save your plan and box.

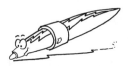

Box Sides

the cereal boxes • drawing paper • scissors • pens, colored pencils, or fine-line markers • glue

Cut two strips of paper to fit the box sides. At the top of one, write "Nourishing Facts About ___(Your Name)___." List things you really want others to know. What are your great personality traits? When were your proudest moments? Which hobbies and interests excite you most? On the other strip, create a coupon. What service can you offer? A drum lesson? Study help? Glue the strips to the sides of your cereal box. Save the box for two more activities.

Box Front

the cereal boxes • kids' photos (optional) • drawing paper • scissors • markers • glue

Tip: Use an instant or a digital camera to take pictures for the box fronts.

The star of this box is you! Make a new front cover on a sheet of paper the size of the box. Add your photo or a drawing of yourself. Design your name in bold, bright letters across the top. Replace the cereal company's logo with your initials, your nickname (if you have one), or a picture or symbol. Glue your sheet to the front of the box. Save the box for three more activities.

Box Back and Top

the cereal boxes • drawing paper • magazines • scissors • markers • glue

Fill the back of the box with a collage celebrating you. Use a sheet of paper the size of the box. Cover it with pictures that show what you like to do. Let your imagination guide you. Cut pictures from magazines, draw, or add a recipe, the words or music to a song, or a special quote. Glue the sheet to the box back. Finish your box by cutting paper for the box top. Add your name, the date, or a slogan. Save the box for one more activity.

TV Ads

the cereal boxes

Think of a cereal ad on TV. Does the ad have a jingle that sticks in your mind? Does it have a slogan? Come up with your own slogan or jingle about the cereal-box you. If you like, volunteer to perform your ad for the class. You're worth promoting, so sell yourself!

Think About It, Talk About It

- You want to stand in a store window and "sell" yourself. How will you show what's best about you?

- What TV game show would you like to be a contestant on? Why do you think you'd be especially good at that game?

Affirmation

I'm worth celebrating!

Resources

For Students

A Life Like Mine: How Children Live Around the World (DK Publishing with UNICEF, 2003). Profiles of 18 children lavishly presented with photos takes readers on a fascinating journey around the world. A celebration of diversity!

Loggins, Kenny. *Yesterday, Today, Tomorrow: The Greatest Hits of Kenny Loggins* (Columbia, Sony Music Entertainment, 1997). Includes many celebratory tunes, including the quiet "Celebrating Me Home" and rowdier boogie tunes like "Footloose" and "I'm All Right." On CD and audiocassette.

Ramón's Cereal Box

Here's the cereal box designed by a boy named Ramón:

What's Important to Me?

"The best things in life aren't things."

Ann Landers, U.S. advice columnist

Looking at what you think is important helps you understand yourself. Certain things, people, and ideas mean something special to you. As you look at why you care about the things you do, you choose and form values. Here's a chance to learn more about who you are—and who you want to be.

"Top Five" List

Make a list of the five most important things in your life. Think about them. Why is each item important? Is there anything on your list that you could live without? That you couldn't? Compare lists with a partner. Did you name any of the same things? Tell your partner why each item on your list means so much to you. Save the list and look at it from time to time. See if what's important changes or stays the same.

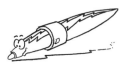

People Poems

copies of handout on page 11 • pens, colored pencils, or markers

Think about a person who's important to you. It might be a grown-up who's helped you with a problem. It might be a friend who likes to do the same things you like to do. It might be a brother or sister who makes you laugh. On the handout, write a poem about the person. Your poem can be short or long and can rhyme or not rhyme. Add some color to your poem page. Share the poem with that special person.

School Walk

Take a walk through the halls of your school. Look at the bulletin boards, trophy cases, and displays. Look into doors and out of windows. What do you see that you like? What would you change if you could? What things about your school are you proud of? What makes you feel like you belong? What else would you like to see on your school walls? Return to your room and talk with classmates about what you like best about your school.

Kindness Role-Plays

Often what's important isn't money or things—it's showing kindness and caring. Can you think of a time when you helped another person? Or when someone was kind to you? Tell a partner about what happened. Listen to your partner's story, too. Together, act out these experiences for others in the class. Talk about why acts of kindness become important memories.

"Business" Cards

sample business cards • 3" x 5" file cards

People use business cards to tell others what they do. Look at a few business cards. They're small, so they tell only a few important things about the person. Design a simple "business" card that tells something important about you. On a file card, print or write your name, nickname (if you have one), address, and phone number. Draw a simple sketch or symbol that represents you. If you like, add a one-liner so others know your specialty (examples: "bike rider," "computer whiz," "collector and painter of plastic figures").

◎ Justin Roberts ◎
234 Fifth Street, Apt. 12B
Brent, KS 66012
913-555-3456
"Justin's my name,
skateboarding's my game!"

Makiko Fumata
1020 Riverbend Road
Homedale, Oregon 97467
555-2229
Ask me about my dog, Zippy

Think About It, Talk About It

- Look up *value* in the dictionary. Explain its meaning as both a verb and a noun.

- Do you think you value the same things that kids valued in the past? What might be the same? What might be different?

- What are some values you learn at home? At school? Which do you think is more important—things or values? Why?

- Who are the people who help you figure out what's important in your life? How do they help you do this?

Affirmation

I am learning about who I am
and what's important to me.

Resource

For Students

Lewis, Barbara A. *What Do You Stand For? For Kids: A Guide to Building Character* (Free Spirit Publishing, 2005). This book invites kids to develop a better understanding of positive character traits such as wisdom, honesty, patience, respect, kindness, and more—and to practice them in their daily lives. Ages 7–12.

For Teachers

A Leader's Guide to What Do You Stand For? For Kids CD-ROM (Free Spirit Publishing, 2005). Eleven lessons reinforce and expand the messages of the student book. Grades 1–6.

People Poem

My Greatest Fears

"To fear is one thing. To let fear grab you by the tail and swing you around is another."

Katherine Paterson, U.S. children's writer, in *Jacob Have I Loved*

Everyone has fears. Though you can't always change the things you fear, you can arm yourself with knowledge and information that help you deal with them. Here are some ideas for putting your fears in perspective.

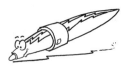

Fear Lists

Make your own private list of the things you fear. Then have volunteers tell some of the things they fear. Write these fears on the board. Look at the group's list. Talk about it. What are some fears many people in the class share? Has someone found a way to get over a fear? How? What's something you used to be afraid of that's not on the list now? What's on the list now that you weren't afraid of when you were younger? Why and how do fears change as you get older?

Help Lists

Tip: Invite a local weather reporter, school social worker, or community police officer to talk to the class about a fear shared by many in your group.

Knowing how to be safe can help ease some fears. As a group, focus on a weather disaster like an earthquake or a tornado. What do you need to know and do to be safe? Where can you get the information you need? List resources for getting help. Your list might include the school office, the local weather bureau, police and fire stations, TV or radio stations, or the chamber of commerce of a city that's gone through a disaster.

You can get help for other fears, too. Create your own personal list of people and places that can help you deal with things you fear the most.

Fears on TV and in the Movies

copies of handout on page 14 • drawing pencils or fine-line markers

Think of some movies and TV shows that deal with things kids worry about. Talk briefly about how the characters overcome their fears or problems. On the handout, draw a scene from one of the programs. In your drawing, show how the people in the story handled the problem.

Role-Plays

Think about a fear you have overcome. How did you do it? Did you talk to a grown-up or a friend? Did you read a book or see a TV show that helped you think of a way to deal with it? Did you give yourself a pep talk? Form small groups. Decide how to role-play your fears. Talk together to find a solution to handling the fear. Act out the solution so that others can watch and learn.

Sing-Alongs

radio or CD or tape player and music (optional)

Do some rockin' and rollin' to get your fears down to size. Take the song from the musical *South Pacific*, "I'm Gonna Wash That Man Right Outa My Hair." Change the words to "I'm gonna wash that fear right outa my head!" Or try some creative new words for "Yakety Yak," "Purple People Eater," or "Monster Mash." Do you have an idea for a song the group could use? Share it. Sing it and move!

Think About It, Talk About It

- Be a critic. Did a particular book, TV show, movie, or song handle and resolve a fear to your liking? Discuss your thoughts. Rate the story or song on a scale of 1–10.

- Do you feel that adults take your fears seriously? If not, how can you talk to them about this so you can get help?

Affirmation

I can get help to handle my fears.

Resources

For Students

A Child's Celebration of Rock 'N' Roll. (Music for Little People, Warner Bros. Records, 1996). Performed by the original artists, the songs on this recording include "Monster Mash," "Yakety Yak," "Purple People Eater," and more. (Don't let the producer's name stop you from using this resource with older kids. Music for Little People makes tapes and CDs that kids 8–12 and even older will enjoy.) Find the cassette or CD in your local children's book or toy store. Web site: www.musicforlittlepeople.com

Hest, Amy, illustrations by P.J. Lynch. *When Jessie Came Across the Sea* (Candlewick Press, 2003). A touching story of handling fears, told through a brave girl's journey to America alone. Moving, strangers, scary weather, the fear of losing a belonging, the demands of others, and school stress are all presented simply yet clearly in this uplifting tale. A visually appealing book. Ages 4–8.

Fears in the Movies

14

My Greatest Hope

"Keep your eyes on the stars, keep your feet on the ground."
Theodore Roosevelt (1858–1919), 26th U.S. President

Hope leads us to change ourselves and the world for the better. As you look at your hopes, you learn more about what you value. You see that changing your future is up to you. Imagine what *could* be!

Mural of Hopes

white or blue parcel paper • paints and brushes

Tip: For a quick technique with easy cleanup, use small pieces of sponge as applicators and unused Styrofoam meat trays as palettes.

In *The Wizard of Oz*, Dorothy found hope "Somewhere Over the Rainbow." What are your hopes for yourself or the world? A clean environment? World peace? An end to hunger? A cure for cancer? Paint a class mural that shows your hopes for a bright future floating in the sky. Remember, anything is possible. The sky's the limit!

Hopeful Words

Dr. Martin Luther King, Jr. strengthened the Civil Rights movement with his famous words, "I have a dream." In the 1996 Olympics, Gloria Estefan sang, "Reach higher . . . touch the sky . . . be stronger . . . put my spirit to the test." Can you think of other famous sayings or songs with a message of hope? Have the hopes come true? If not, do you think they will? How? Write a short phrase or sentence that expresses your own hope for yourself, your community, or the world. Share your words of hope and talk about what you can do to help make them happen.

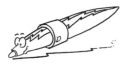

School Letter

Take a look at your school. Are you proud of it? Are you happy with all that goes on? Do you have ideas for making it a better place? As a group or individually, write a letter to your principal, dean, or school board. Tell your greatest hopes for your school, now and for the future. Suggest ways to make the hopes become realities.

Clean-up Time

You can only hope for a better you, family, school, and world if you look to yourself first. *You* can make a difference. Start today by picking up the little pieces of your life. Look at your classroom, desk, or backpack. Gather up the little things that have gone astray. Put papers, pencils, books, and games in their place. Recycle those empty soda cans and juice bottles. Throw away that garbage. Caring for yourself and the things around you is hope in action.

 **Letters for Sick Kids**

drawing or writing paper • colored pencils and markers • small envelopes • 1 large envelope • first-class postage stamps (optional)

Tip: Glitter can be a problem in hospitals, so don't use glitter to decorate the letters.

Share hope by sending a message of cheer to sick kids. Make your message fun or funny. Tell a joke, pose a riddle, draw a humorous picture, or relate a funny story about yourself. Avoid saying "Get well soon." Instead, keep your message focused on cheer and humor. When you're done, put your letter in an unsealed envelope. If you can, include a postage stamp for your letter. Send the messages in one large envelope to a local children's hospital.

 Think About It, Talk About It

- Is it important to take time to think about what you want for yourself, your family, your school, and your world? Why?

- Do you know people whose hopes have helped them or others? Give examples.

- Who are some well-known people whose hopes and dreams have led them to work for change? What did they do? What happened because of them?

 Affirmation

Hope is a word I can act on.
It can light the way for a bright tomorrow.

 **Resources**

For Students

Espeland, Pamela, and Rosemary Wallner. *Making the Most of Today* (Free Spirit Publishing, 1998). Daily readings and quotations to direct young people into hopeful thinking and choice-making. Ages 11 and up.

My Favorite Memories

"Memory is the diary we all carry about with us."
Mary H. Waldrip, U.S. journalist

Memories bring you joy, wisdom, and experiences you can share with others. Holding onto memories keeps you in touch with moments that have shaped your life. It's time to rediscover what's important in your past.

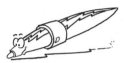

Memory Stories

Do you remember a favorite old pair of shoes? A report you were proud of? A friend who moved away? A toy you loved when you were small? Take a few minutes to search your mind for a lost memory—a treasure that you miss. Write a story or poem that tells why the memory is so important to you.

Memory Book Pages

drawing paper • pens, colored pencils, or fine-line markers • 3-ring notebook and hole punch (optional)

What do you want to be remembered for? A sense of humor? A special talent? Your kindness to others? Your love of animals? Think of a phrase or sentence that describes your best qualities. Write it—in your own unique way—on a sheet of drawing paper. Add doodles, decorations, or more words that fit this description of you. Share your page with a friend, or put it with your classmates' pages into a memory book.

Memories in Your Backpack

drawing paper • drawing pencils

Grab your pack or bag and dig down. What do you find buried at the very bottom? Choose one item that has been forgotten beneath your books and papers. Draw a pencil sketch that gives new importance to this lost piece of your life. Give your sketch a name (examples: "In memory of the pen that died," "In memory of the snack that got away"). If you have time, add a brief story or remembrance about your item.

Return a Good Deed

Recall a time someone was kind to you. Think about how good it made you feel. How can you let the person know that the kindness made a memory for you? Think of a way to give some kindness back. Will you write a note? Lend a hand? Offer a hug? Make a plan.

Memory Dances

Look through your own memories or your teacher's to come up with a short list of old dance steps. Who can break dance? Who knows how to jitterbug, polka, twist, swing, cha-cha, or limbo? Who can do the hora, mashed potato, or macarena? Try a few steps with a partner or on your own.

Think About It, Talk About It

- Why are memories important?

- What makes a lasting memory?

- How far back can you remember? What helps you remember?

- Journals, pictures, souvenirs, and storytellers help keep memories alive. How can some of these help you hold onto your memories?

Affirmation

Memories help me hold onto important people and things in my life.

Resources

For Students

Keehm, Sally M. *I Am Regina* (Putnam Publishing Group, 2001). In 1755, Regina is captured by Allegheny Indians and held for more than nine years. Her childhood memories of growing up white fade as her memories and experience of living as a Native American grow more vivid. Together, these memories become the threads that bind her life together and help her reach her destiny. Ages 9–12.

Reeder, Carolyn. *Shades of Gray* (Aladdin, 1999). Will Page is left an orphan by the Civil War. While living with his Uncle Jed's family, Will often recalls his comfortable life before the war. These memories give Will strength and comfort to go forward. Ages 9–12.

Proud to Be Me

"Self-esteem—that's really the most important thing."
Staci Keanan, U.S. actress

Everyone needs a healthy sense of self-esteem. To build your self-esteem, take a look deep inside at what's unique and special about you. Find what you're proud of, and express it!

"Today's Special" Signs

copies of handout on page 21 • colored pencils or markers

By looking into a store window, you get an idea of what's inside. What do you see and feel inside *you*? Use the "Today's Special" handout to create a store window display about yourself. Add a sign listing a few of the best, most interesting, or most important things about you. Include pictures and colors to show yourself off in style!

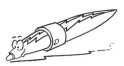

Radio Announcements

A store or business that's proud of a new product announces it to the world. What can you announce? Did you pass that tough test and get a grade you're proud of? Invite the new kid in school to join you at lunch? Speak up at your club meeting? Play the trombone in a recital? Describe what you did in a brief radio script. Grab a microphone and read your announcement to a friend.

Nick Romowski proudly announces that he aced last Friday's pop quiz in geography. What's the secret to his success? Nick credits his new study plan and his use of the class computer to travel the globe on the Web. Congratulations to Nick on a job well done!

Flag Cheers

construction paper • tape • Popsicle sticks •
copies of handout on page 22

Choose two sheets of construction paper for making two flags. Tape a Popsicle stick to one side of each flag. While you work, think of a word or two that describes you—like "singer," "friendly," or "science whiz." Then look at the *semaphore* (flag signal) alphabet on the handout. Figure out how to use your flags to signal the words that describe you. Do your cheer! Watch your classmates do theirs. End the activity by raising all those flags in a flutter.

You on a Poster

posterboard or drawing paper • markers

Tip: Book or movie posters give a firsthand look at poster art. Many are free for the asking at bookstores or video rental shops.

Think of three reasons why you like being *you*. Write them down. Use those three reasons to create a bold poster advertising yourself. Make your poster simple and bright to catch people's attention. Use a few choice words that capture your terrific qualities. Have your poster ready to make its debut in the window of your classroom or home. Advertise the best you.

Self-Talk

"Self-talk" is what you say *to* yourself *about* yourself. Positive self-talk boosts self-esteem. Find a partner. Help each other think of positive self-talk for getting through hard situations. (Examples: "Way to go! I really studied, and it paid off!" "This song sounds a little better every time I play it.") Write down your partner's ideas and your

own. Keep your notes on helpful self-talk and add to them when more words come to mind.

Think About It, Talk About It

• Why is it important to like yourself?

• What things do you do to feel good about yourself?

• Young people often look to their friends for approval. How can the approval of others help you? How can it hurt?

Affirmation

I'm proud of who I am and who I'm becoming.

Resources

For Students

Venezia, Mike. *Henri De Toulouse-Lautrec* (Childrens Press, 1995). Learn about this French painter and about poster art in a fun way. Toulouse-Lautrec was known for the advertising art he created. His poster techniques continue to inspire us today. Ages 4–8.

For Teachers

Borba, Michele. *Esteem Builders: A K–8 Self-Esteem Curriculum for Improving Student Achievement, Behavior and School Climate* (Jalmar, 2003). It contains over 250 activities that cross-correlate to all subject areas and grade levels.

My Personal Portfolio

"We are the hero of our own story."

Mary Therese McCarthy (1912–1989), U.S. writer, critic, and educator

There are many kinds of portfolios. A family portfolio holds photos, vacation souvenirs, favorite recipes, or the family tree. A work portfolio showcases talents and skills to get a job. A personal portfolio offers a unique way to look at yourself and at how you want others to see you. It also lets you see the things you've accomplished and the ways you've grown. Create a personal student portfolio to showcase your best self.

Note: Do the first four "My Personal Portfolio" activities in sequence.

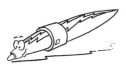

Portfolio Plan

folders for the portfolios • copies of handout on page 25

A *portfolio* is a kind of album or scrapbook. Here's your chance to plan your own student portfolio—a showcase for your best schoolwork, your interests and hobbies, and the ways you help others. Use the "Planning My Portfolio" handout to decide how to put together your portfolio. It should include only a few items—the very best of your best! Think about what essay, test, or other school paper you will use to create your first portfolio page. Plan to have that on hand for the next activity. Keep your planning page in your portfolio folder. Use it as you put your portfolio together.

Schoolwork Page

the portfolio folders • school papers for the portfolios • colored construction paper • glue • scissors • pens or fine-line markers

Glue the school paper you selected to a sheet of colored paper. Allow space for a small label that includes the title, date, and a few simple words to explain your work. Make the small label from a different-colored sheet. Use the dictionary to ensure perfect spelling. Write neatly. Glue the label in place. Voilà! The first page of your personal portfolio is complete. Plan to mount and describe each new page in the same way.

A Second Page

the portfolio folders • drawing paper • colored pencils or markers • colored construction paper • glue • scissors • pens or fine-line markers

Draw a picture that shows something other than schoolwork that you want to highlight in your portfolio. You might show a hobby, a way you help others, or a club or group you're proud to be part of. If drawing is your hobby or interest, select a favorite drawing and use it to create this page. Mount and label the page in the same way you did your schoolwork page.

Present Your Portfolio

the portfolio folders

Volunteer to present your portfolio out loud. If you're nervous, take a few deep breaths to steady yourself. Get a drink of water if you need one. Then stand up and speak proudly as you show and explain your portfolio to your classmates.

School Portfolio

drawing paper • colored pencils or markers • folder to hold the school portfolio

Tip: Photocopy the pages and make several portfolios. Share them with newcomers or send a copy along when someone moves away.

Make a portfolio that shows off your school. As a group, make a quick list of what you can show (examples: the cafeteria with its famous pizza burgers, the custodian who loves to swap stories, the computer lab where you link up with another school). Choose one of the ideas and work alone or with a partner to make a page. Write a sentence or two telling why kids like this feature of your school. Make a small drawing to go with it. Label and date the page. Put the pages together in a book or folder called "A Few Cool Views of Our School."

Think About It, Talk About It

- Do you think creating a portfolio is a good way to review and share your life with others? What are some other ways to remember accomplishments and good times?

- Portfolios can come in any size or shape. What are some other types of portfolios you could make?

Affirmation

My personal portfolio lets me show others what I'm proud of.

Resources

For Students

Brewster, Hugh. *Anastasia's Album* (Hyperion, 1997). An intimate look at the life of Anastasia Romanov, the youngest daughter of the last Russian czar, through photographs, keepsakes, and letters. Note the author's approach of a family portfolio with a consistent and organized format. Ages 9–12.

Kimeldorf, Martin. *Creating Portfolios for Success in School, Work, and Life* (Free Spirit Publishing, 1994). Learn the techniques for creating portfolios for personal, student, project, or professional use. They serve as tools for self-discovery. Ages 11 and up.

For Teachers

Kimeldorf, Martin. *A Teacher's Guide to Creating Portfolios for Success in School, Work, and Life* Life (Free Spirit Publishing, 1994). This companion guide to the student book suggests ways to implement and evaluate portfolios at various grade levels and adapt them for students with special needs.

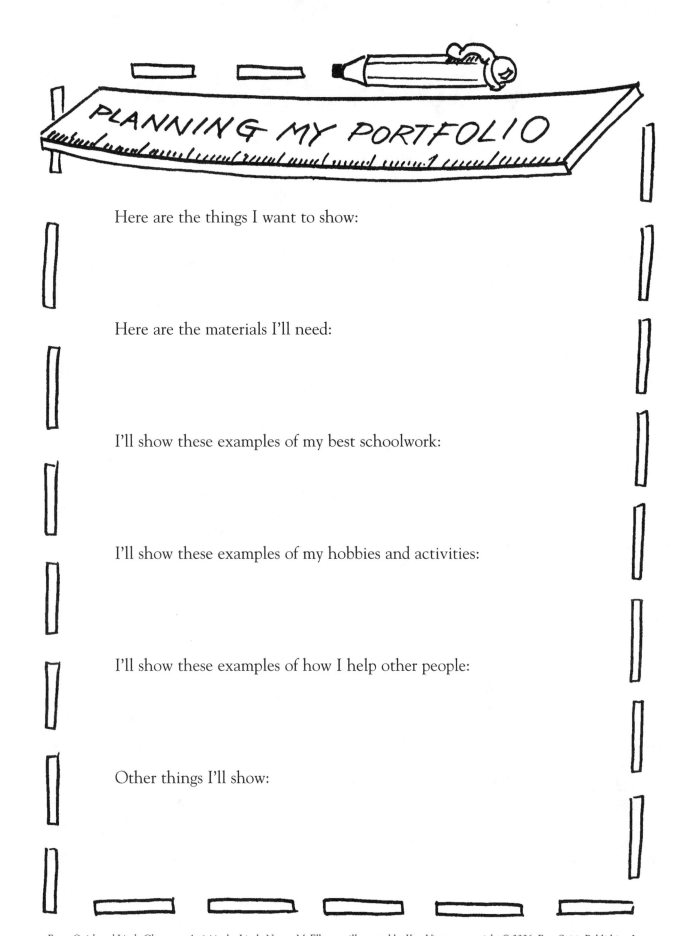

PLANNING MY PORTFOLIO

Here are the things I want to show:

Here are the materials I'll need:

I'll show these examples of my best schoolwork:

I'll show these examples of my hobbies and activities:

I'll show these examples of how I help other people:

Other things I'll show:

My Special Talent

"We can't take credit for our talents. It's how we use them that counts."

Madeleine L'Engle, U.S. author

Each of us has a talent for something. Recognizing that talent is the first step toward developing it. Let's go on a talent search!

Note: Do the "My Special Talent" activities in sequence.

 ## Talent Talks

Talents come in many forms. Some people are natural athletes, musicians, or comedians. Others have a special ability to get along with animals or to listen and understand what someone else is feeling. Still others are skilled at solving puzzles or creating stories and games. As a group, make a list of different kinds of talents. What talents do you see among yourselves? Among your friends and families? Make your list as long as you can. When you're done, think about what your own special talent might be.

 ## Talent Charades

Do you have a talent that you use and work on every day? Are you looking for the talent that's still hidden inside you? Tell the story of a talent you have or want to develop. Instead of naming your talent, use pantomime. Be physical and expressive. See how long it takes others to guess where your talent lies.

 ## A Plan to Build Your Talent

copies of handout on page 28

What are you doing to build your talent? Do you take lessons? Practice? Does someone encourage or help you? Do you have a plan that you follow? Do you want to start a plan? On the handout, write a five-step plan for developing and strengthening your talent. Save your plan for the next activity.

 ## A Picture of Your Plan

plans from preceding activity • sheets of 8½" x 11" paper • colored pencils or markers

Review your five-step plan for developing your talent. Draw a picture that shows something about your talent. You might show yourself doing one of the steps or sharing your talent with someone else. Save your drawing and your plan for one more activity.

 ## Talent Plan Book

plans and drawings from preceding activities • 12" x 18" piece of cardboard or posterboard for the book's cover • tape • 2 lengths of ribbon (18" each)

Tip: For a finished look, have volunteers illustrate the cover.

Turn your plan pages into a class book. For the cover, fold a piece of cardboard as shown in the drawing below. Open the cover and tape the edge of someone's written plan (face up) to the inside-cover spine. Tape the edge of the drawing that goes with the plan to the other edge of the written plan. Continue taping plans and drawings. Fold the pages of the book accordion-style. Tape ribbon to the inside edges of the cover, close the book, and tie it in front. Keep your class talent plan book with other important classroom reference materials. Look at the book often. Follow through on your plan to develop your special talent.

 ## Think About It, Talk About It

- Does talent take patience and practice, or does it just happen naturally? Give examples of talented individuals—famous or not—to support your answer.

- What suggestions would you give a teacher or parent to help you strengthen your talent?

- What can you do if someone tells you that you have no talent? Or that someone "like you" can't do something?

 ## Affirmation

I have a special talent that I can work on and take pride in.

 ## Resources

For Students

Cummings, Pat, ed. *Talking with Artists,* vol. 1–3 (Simon & Schuster Books for Young Readers, 1995). Favorite illustrators of kids' books tell how they developed their talent as children, answer questions about their work, and show their secret techniques for drawing. Ages 9–12.

For Teachers

Cleveland, Lisa and Katie Wood Ray. *About the Authors: Writing Workshop with Our Youngest Writers* (Heinemann, 2004). Encourage your young students to discover their creativity through writing.

My Five-Step Talent Plan

The talent I want to develop is _____.

These are the five steps I'll follow to develop my talent:

1.

2.

3.

4.

5.

My Favorite Hobby

"Tell me and I forget, teach me and I remember, involve me and I learn."

Benjamin Franklin (1706–1790), American statesman and philosopher

Hobbies give you a change of focus from your daily routine. Often, they offer a chance to learn a wealth of new skills and to share enjoyable time with family and friends. You might have a hobby that you're not even aware of. Think about the things you do for relaxation. Is there something you like to do often? You may have found a hobby! Take time to explore some of the different hobbies of people in your class.

Note: Do the first two "My Favorite Hobby" activities in sequence.

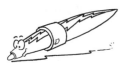 ## Hobby Recipe

copies of handout on page 31 • scissors

There's a recipe card just waiting to be filled with clues about your favorite hobby, activity, or collection. Look at the sample recipes. Fill in and cut out your own. Give plenty of hints, but leave *off* your name and the name of your hobby. Give this card your best effort. Save it along with everyone else's for the next activity.

 ## Guess the Hobbies

recipe cards from preceding activity

Pick one of the hobby recipe cards. If you draw your own, return it to the pile and draw again. Read the recipe to yourself. Think what hobby it might be. When your turn comes, read it aloud, and guess the hobby name, if you can. Then guess who the "cook"—the recipe author—might be. Have the "cook" stand up, take credit, and answer questions about the hobby.

 ## Hobby Words

drawing paper • colored pencils or fine-line markers • decorative materials and glue (optional)

Write the name of your hobby in capital letters along the left side of a sheet of drawing paper. For each letter, think of a word that begins with that letter and describes something about the hobby. Add drawings or decorations to complete your hobby word page. Display the pages on a bulletin board for all to see.

Rhythm
And
Poetry
My style of music
U should try it!
Speak, don't sing
Imagination needed
Come rap with me

Hobby Collages

drawing paper • magazines • scissors • glue • markers

Form groups of three or four and take turns briefly describing your hobbies. Then work together to cut and glue pictures from magazines or draw pictures that represent the hobbies of people in your group. While you work, think and talk about the answers to these questions:

- How did you get started in your hobby?
- Who helps you or takes part in your hobby with you?
- How do you show your hobby to others?

When you're finished, have a volunteer show your group's collage to the class and explain how you've represented the different hobbies.

Sharing a Hobby

Think about an activity you like to do with your father, mother, or another adult. Why do you enjoy doing the activity with this person? Why do you think the other person enjoys doing it with you? Do you consider the activity a hobby? Write a very short note asking the person to take some time to enjoy this hobby together.

Think About It, Talk About It

- A friend says a toy you play with is babyish. A classmate says a school club you're in is stupid. Would calling that interest a "hobby" ease the teasing? How can you help others see the value that an interest holds for you?

- Name different hobbies, and explain what a person might learn from each of them.

- Do you have a hobby that you do with a parent, a grandparent, or another adult? Share it with the group.

Affirmation

My favorite hobby brings me pleasure, knowledge, and a chance to spend time with other people.

Resources

Note: Many books that target specific hobbies can be found at your local library or bookstore.

For Students

Boys' Life. Published by the Boy Scouts of America, this magazine is one all kids—boys and girls alike—will enjoy. Monthly issues contain columns on such topics as collecting, hobbies, and sports. For subscription information, visit www.boyslife.org

George, Jean Craighead. *There's an Owl in the Shower* (Harper Trophy, 1997). A boy and his father who become involved in an owl's well-being find their relationship and their attitudes transformed. The story shows how a shared interest can grow into a hobby. Ages 9–12.

Oswald, Diane, illustrations by Brent Roderick. *101 Great Collectibles for Kids* (Antique Trader Books, 1997). An interesting, appealing, and comprehensive book that helps children get started collecting books, puzzles, photographs, pens, holiday items, refrigerator magnets, stuffed animals, and many other things. Ages 9–12.

Recipe for _____

What you need:
magnifying glass, tweezers, album

What you do:
Cut items from envelope.
Soak in warm water.
Use tweezers to remove items from envelope paper. Let dry, then mount in album.

Hints:
I can get some of these items from catalogs or the post office. Some come to me in the mail.

Name _____

Recipe for _____

What you need:
round object (often orange), ring with net attached, plastic board

What you do:
bounce the object, run with it, throw it to someone else, try to throw it into the ring

Hints:
You don't have to be tall, but it helps!

Name _____

Recipe for _____

What you need:

What you do:

Hints:

Name _____

My Promise to Myself

"If it is to be, it is up to me."
Shirley Nelson Hutton, U.S. businesswoman

A promise is a commitment. What you wish for today can become a goal for tomorrow. Before you can make a personal promise, you need to imagine what you can do and be. As you explore what you want for yourself and the world, you gain new insights into the meaning of personal responsibility. Make a promise you can keep.

A Perfect Day

drawing paper • colored pencils or markers

Imagine a day that's perfect from start to finish. Where would you go? What would you do? Who would you do it with? Draw a picture of this perfect day. Share it with a partner. How is your partner's perfect day like yours? How is it different?

Shoe-Box Game

shoe box and lid; cut a hand-sized hole in the side of the box

Tip: Extra props (toy cars, building blocks, doll clothes, etc.) can make this activity more fun.

Look around the room, your backpack, and your desk. Find some small thing that represents your future career. Be creative! Do you want to be an architect? Choose a building block or a ruler and sheet of paper. A geologist? A simple rock will do. A travel agent? Look for a map or a toy airplane. Keep your item secret and hidden. Put it in the box—don't let anyone see it! Pass the box around the circle. Others will feel your item and try to guess what career you have in mind.

Pie Chart

copies of handout on page 34

You've hit the jackpot! You've won a month off from school and the chance to do and explore whatever you want. Your jackpot has a single rule: In one month, you must report back to a judge about your worthwhile activities. What are the things you would really like to do and try? Use the pie chart on the handout to divide up your activities. Label each part. What worthwhile things will you do with all your time?

Past Hopes and Dreams

Imagine you've found a box in the back of the closet. Inside the box is a promise you wrote to yourself three years ago. What does the note say? Think back three years. How old were you? What kinds of dreams and hopes did you have? What did you want to do? To have? To be? Write that note from long ago. How is your promise different from one you would write about today? Do you still have the same hopes and dreams? Share your note or keep it private—it's up to you.

Personal Promise

paper • pens, pencils, or fine-line markers

Make a promise to yourself. What one thing will you do to make you a better person or the world a better place? Why do you want to do it? How will you make it happen? How will you get around problems that stand in the way? Who can help you reach your goal? Write your promise and your plans on a sheet of paper. Keep your promise in a place where you will read it often—taped inside your locker or on your closet door.

Think About It, Talk About It

- One way to keep personal promises is to write them down in a journal. What are some other ways to make and keep promises to yourself?

- Is it important to think about your future now, while you're young? Why or why not?

- How can you figure out what you want to do or become?

Affirmation

Making a promise to myself
gives me something to work toward.

Resources

For Students

Cushman, Karen. *Catherine, Called Birdy* (Harper Trophy, 1995). Birdy, who lives during medieval times, wants to be a painter, a peddler, a crusader, and more. Though Birdy's goals don't match her father's wishes, her spirit and dreams lead her to please both herself and her father. Ages 11 and up.

Paulsen, Gary. *Hatchet* (Simon Pulse, 1999). In this 1988 Newbery Honor Book, thirteen-year-old Brian is the sole survivor of a plane crash in the Canadian wilderness. He promises himself he will survive the ordeal, and the book details his efforts to do so over fifty-four challenging and exhausting days. Two later books by Paulsen, *The River* (Yearling Books, 1991) and *Brian's Winter* (Laurel-Leaf Books, 1998), continue and retell Brian's story. Ages 9–12.

For Teachers

Benson, Peter L., Judy Galbraith, and Pamela Espeland. *What Kids Need to Succeed* (Free Spirit Publishing, 1998). By learning about the forty proven developmental assets that promote success and prevent at-risk behavior in kids, parents and teachers can find ways to make and keep a personal promise to help their children lead healthy, productive lives.

Dividing My Time

Getting
to Know
Others

Who Are You?

"The most important fact about Spaceship Earth: an instruction book didn't come with it."
Buckminster Fuller (1895–1983), U.S. engineer and inventor

Learning about others requires more than curiosity. It calls for skills like meeting, greeting, asking questions, listening, and sharing information. Sometimes it calls for imagination as well. Let's practice some of these skills with a new twist—getting to know beings from another planet!

Universal Greetings

Around the globe, humans greet each other with a bow, a curtsy, a handshake, or a "high five." Imagine yourself meeting a being from another planet. What form of greeting would you use to offer a friendly hello? Find a partner and invent a greeting. Share your universal greetings with others.

Descriptive Names

The name of a spaceship describes the craft's mission: "Probe," "Explorer," or "Orbiter." Team up with a partner. Try to find out what your partner feels are his or her most important traits or interests. Then come up with a word or phrase to go with your partner's name. The term should help others learn more about who your partner is. (Examples: "Libby—Computer Guru," "Darnell—Wordsmith," "Joe—Spider Man," "Kara—Asker of Many Questions.")

Picture Greetings

colored pencils or markers • picture of NASA space probe message (optional—see "Resources," page 37)

For space travel, scientists have come up with a picture greeting to give to alien beings. The picture is meant to show who we earthlings are and where we come from. What would you want an alien to know about you? How would you show friendliness? Draw your friendly greeting. Team up with three or four other people and talk about what the different picture greetings say.

Universal Questions

Imagine that you're working at a space control center here on Earth. Your job is to develop a manual with questions to ask space beings so you can learn more about them. What do you want to learn? How can you politely ask about those things? Write your questions. Try them out on classmates. (Examples: "What brings you to our planet?" "What is the distance between your home and mine?")

Group Logo

colored pencils or markers

Like a truck or an airplane, a spacecraft is marked with a *logo*—a picture or design that tells something about where the craft comes from. Team up with four or five classmates. Imagine that your group will be traveling together in space. You need a logo for your spacecraft that tells something about all of you. Talk together and find out something you have in common. Do you all have a sense of humor? Love chocolate ice cream? Dream of living on a space station? Come up with one shared trait or interest that connects you as a group. Together, design a logo for your group. Share your logo with the other groups. Can others guess what the logo says about you?

carefully carry the world

friendship

Think About It, Talk About It

- When he took office, Thomas Jefferson ended the practice of people bowing to the U. S. president. Instead, he encouraged handshakes. What does this tell you about President Jefferson? About American government?

- What forms of greeting are you most comfortable with? Why?

- When you meet another kid for the first time, what kinds of questions do you like to ask? Why?

- There's a saying, "Actions speak louder than words." Do you think it's true? Why or why not? Would you change the saying? How?

Affirmation

By meeting, greeting, and getting to know someone else, I learn.

Resources

For Students

Ash, Russell. *The World in One Day* (DK Publishing, 1997). You'll find a picture of the NASA space probe message on page 26.

E.T.: The Extra-Terrestrial (Universal Studios, 1982). E.T. is a lovable space creature left behind by his own kind on Earth. A young boy befriends him, and together they learn about each other. Rated PG.

Kids Discover. A monthly kids' magazine that explores a new topic in detail in each issue. *Kids Discover* has won two Parents' Choice Gold Awards. For subscription information, visit www.kidsdiscover.com

Getting to Know You

"Why not go out on a limb? Isn't that where the fruit is?"
Frank Scully, U.S. author

Friendship develops when we take the time and effort to get to know someone. First impressions might not give the whole picture—or the right one. Here's a chance to get to know some of your classmates a little better.

Note: Do the "Getting to Know You" activities in sequence.

 ## "Personals" Ads

slips of paper, each with a different number • copies of handout on page 40

Teacher: Give each student a number. Tell students to hide the number in their desk or backpack. Keep your own list of students' numbers. *Students:* Newspapers have a section called "Personals." This is a place where people advertise for friends with similar interests. Write your own "Personals" ad. When you're done, put your number (not your name!) on the back of your paper. Keep the number a secret. Collect the ads and save them for the next activity.

 ## Choosing Ads

ads from preceding activity

Without looking, choose a page from the pile of "Personals" ads. One at a time, read the ads aloud. Listen for an ad that describes someone you'd like to get to know. Ask to have that ad. (Draw straws or flip a coin if more than one person wants the ad.) Save the ads for the next activity.

 ## Meeting the Ad Writers

ads from preceding activity

It's time to reveal whose number is whose. Meet with the person whose ad you selected. Spend five minutes learning more about what you have in common and how you're different. Then spend five minutes with the person who chose your ad. (If this is the same person you just talked to, take time to get to know each other a bit better.)

 ## Triptychs

colored pencils or fine-line markers

A *triptych* is a set of three pictures side by side. Think about the person whose ad you chose. Draw a triptych using one of these themes:

- 3 things you and the person have in common
- 3 things you might do together
- 3 ways you're different
- 3 things that really surprised you about the person
- 3 things you really like about the person.

Charades

Team up with the person who chose your ad. Quickly plan a charade that shows something you both like to do. Perform your charade for the rest of the class. Remember, speaking isn't allowed! Have fun guessing other people's charades, too.

Think About It, Talk About It

- What things surprised you about the other person? What's something you especially like about the person?

- What are some ways people are different from each other? How can differences help make a good friendship?

- Do you think it's important to get to know lots of different people? Why or why not?

Affirmation

Getting to know someone can lead me to learn and try new things.

Resources

For Students

King-Smith, Dick. *Babe, the Gallant Pig* (Knopf Books for Young Readers; 2005). Letting "Pig" demonstrate his abilities—which resemble those of a dog—shows others that by getting to know someone, they may be surprised and might learn and try new things. Ages 9–12. The book was adapted as a movie, *Babe* (Universal City Studios, 1995), rated G.

Kid Seeking Classmate to Share Interests and Good Times

_____-grade student wants to get to know someone who enjoys _____, _____, and _____.

My friends like me because:

Here are some of my all-time favorites:

movie   animal

book   subject

food   pastime

sport   season

song   holiday

game   color

My idea of a perfect day is:

Here's something most people don't know about me:

Making Friends

"A friend is a present you give yourself."
Robert Louis Stevenson (1850–1894), Scottish author

It's no secret—we all need friends. Trying to make a new friend can feel scary. It helps to know that most people share this worry at one time or another. Let's look at what friendship means and explore some ways to make new friends.

Friendship Game

Quickly plan a simple game the whole class can enjoy right now, such as "Simon Says," charades, or an alphabet word game. Play the game with two goals in mind: that everyone should have a turn and have fun. What can you do to make sure this happens? After playing the game, discuss how games help people form friendships.

Brainstorming School Friends

What if you were the new kid in school? What if you were in a class with people you'd never met before? What if you felt like "branching out" a little? Brainstorm ways to get a friendship rolling at school. Share all the ideas you can think of, serious or funny—with brainstorming, every thought counts. When you're through, read the list to yourself. Choose an idea that might work for you. Give it a try!

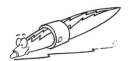

Rules for a Friendship Club

Imagine that you're setting up a friendship club in your town, neighborhood, or apartment building. What kind of club do you want it to be? What will you do? Will you set up your club based on interests and hobbies? Are you thinking big, for many casual pals? Or small, for a close few? What kind of club would help you and others make friends easily? Outline the rules of a club that would be just right for you. Compare notes and see how others would plan their clubs.

Yearbook Mural

butcher paper • colored chalk • tape

Getting involved in school activities is a sure way to make friends. Create a "yearbook mural" that shows how friendships grow at school. Draw large squares that will be the "pages" of your yearbook. Fill in the pages with words, names, and quick sketches of you and others at school. Tape the mural to a wall for all to enjoy. Leave room to add to it as you get more ideas.

Olympic Flag Mosaics

copies of handout on page 43 • various colored or textured papers (newspaper, brown bags, scraps of wrapping paper) • scissors • glue • several sheets of posterboard (at least 12" x 18")

Tip: For efficiency, first cut the paper, then apply glue across the entire surface of the ring, and then drop the paper scraps in place.

The flag of the Olympic Games shows five interlocking rings. The rings represent friendship among the five major areas of the world—Asia, Africa, the Americas, Europe, and Australia. Create Olympic flags to show the interlocking friendships among all the people in your class. Work with a partner to decorate the ring in the handout. Glue small cut pieces of paper inside the circle to form a simple *mosaic* pattern. Cut out your ring. Then join four other pairs of students and glue the five rings on posterboard to create a flag. Step back and admire the flags—and the spirit of friendship they stand for!

Think About It, Talk About It

- Sometimes people want to make friends so much that they make up stories or act like someone they're not. Do you think this can be a good way to make friends? Why or why not?

- It can be hard to make new friends when you move or switch to a new school. Do you know any songs, movies, books, or TV shows that address this issue? How do they deal with it? What do you think of these ideas about making friends?

- Writing letters can develop a friendship. Do you have a pen pal? Would you like one? What are the good and bad points of this type of friendship?

- What things help strengthen a friendship? What things can weaken a friendship?

Affirmation

I can make friends and be a friend.

Resources

For Students

Dierks, Leslie. *Making Mosaics* (Sterling Lark, 2004). Although mosaics appear complex, this book demonstrates how relatively easy they are to create. Includes designs, techniques, and projects. All ages.

Skolsky, Mindy Warshaw. *Love from Your Friend, Hannah* (Harper Trophy, 1999). When Hannah's best friend moves away, Hannah finds new friends by writing letters. Most surprising to her is the gradual discovery that a "dopey" pen pal from Kansas—a boy who at first seems to have little in common with her—becomes a true friend. Ages 9–12.

For Teachers

Student Letter Exchange. Connects kids ages 9–19 with others from around the country or the globe. Write to Student Letter Exchange, 211 Broadway, Suite 201, Lynbrook, NY 11563. Telephone: (516) 887-8628. Web site: www.pen-pal.com

Friendship Ring

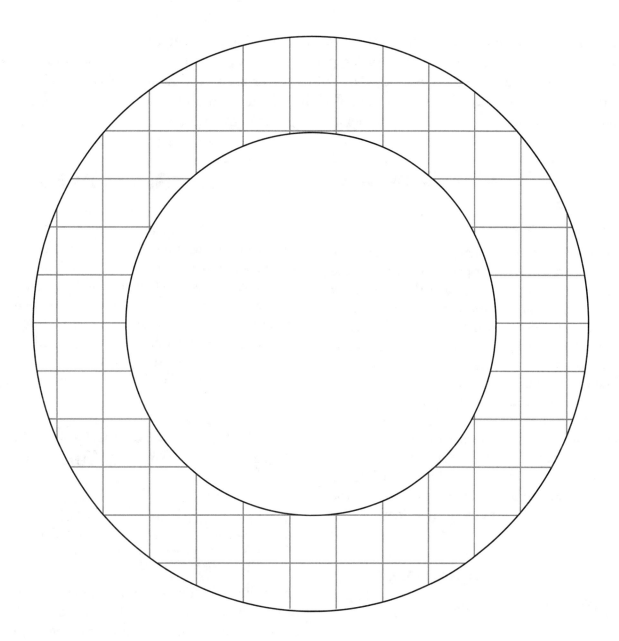

A Walk in Your Shoes

"You cannot put the same shoe on every foot."

Publilius Syrus, Latin dramatist and writer of maxims, 1st century A.D.

Shoes can provide us with an interesting way to learn about ourselves and others. We learn *empathy*—true understanding of another person—by putting ourselves in someone else's shoes. At the same time, we learn that often it's better *not* to follow in someone else's footsteps, and that our own shoes fit us best. Walking in our own and others' shoes allows us to take steps toward empathy and self-understanding. Let's start walking!

Shoe Drawings

drawing paper • pencils

Take off your shoe and draw it. Try the technique of *contouring*, where your pencil never leaves the page and your eyes never leave the shoe. Look closely, draw fast, and have fun. Don't worry if your sketch doesn't seem to match the actual shoe. Sign your name in the lower right-hand corner. Now trade drawings with a partner. Look closely at your partner's drawing. What does the shoe and the way it's drawn tell you about this person? Think of a title for the drawing that fits the person and the shoe (examples: "Going in the Right Direction," "Always Running," or "Who Needs Laces?"). Get your own drawing back again. If you want, add your partner's title idea to the lower left-hand corner of your shoe drawing.

Follow the Leader

Take a walk. Let your steps follow the leader's. March, skip, shuffle, tiptoe, change stride, and take baby steps and giant steps. After a minute, switch to a new leader. Continue changing leaders and walking for about ten minutes. Did every leader move in the same way? How did it feel to follow in someone's footsteps?

Group Skits

Have you ever had a pair of shoes that didn't fit right? Did your feet hurt? Did you get blisters? Did it feel good to have some extra room? Sometimes we try out actions or behaviors that don't quite fit right, either. Have you ever tried to make friends or impress people by acting in a way that didn't really fit you? Did it work? What happened? Act out in small groups what you learned—good or bad—from trying to be like someone else.

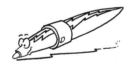

Charting What Shoes Tell Us

copies of handout on page 46

Tip: Visit a local history museum or cultural center. Learn about how and why people developed cultural differences based on their environment, climate, and beliefs. Check out their shoes!

Shoes tell a story. By looking at a shoe, you can tell many things: The climate and landscape in which it's worn. The age group or gender of the wearer. The culture or customs of the shoe's owner. Look at the shoes on the handout. Fill in the chart to show something that each shoe tells you. Imagine yourself wearing one of the different shoes. What would you do? With whom? How would it feel to be living the life that goes with that shoe?

Someone Else's Shoes

There's an expression "to walk in someone else's shoes." Talk about what this means. Then get in small groups and choose one of the following situations. Act out the scene. Trade parts, and act it out again. Each time, think of the person you're pretending to be. How would you feel? What would you do? What would you want others to do?

- You trip and fall, dropping your books and papers all over the floor of the school bus. The other kids laugh.
- Teams are choosing sides and you're the last one picked. As you walk over to join the group, one kid says, "Oh, no—we'll lose for sure now!"
- Someone you really like has a party and doesn't invite you.
- You're eating lunch with your friends. Someone you're in band with asks to sit with you. You know your other friends don't like this person.

Think About It, Talk About It

- When is it good to want to be like someone else? When is it bad?

- What can you learn from putting yourself in someone else's shoes?

- What are some ways to find out how someone else is feeling?

Affirmation

I can understand others by putting myself in their shoes. Though I'll try on many shoes, my own fit me best!

Resources

For Students

Fleischman, Sid, illustrations by Peter Sis. *The Whipping Boy* (Harper Trophy, 2003). When Prince Brat and Jemmy, the prince's "whipping boy," run away from the castle, their identities are mistakenly reversed. Through the experience, the prince develops empathy for his whipping boy, while Jemmy learns to appreciate the benefits he had at the castle. A 1987 Newbery Medal winner. Ages 7–10.

See page 10 for information about *What Do You Stand For? For Kids* by Barbara A. Lewis.

Shoes, Shoes, Shoes

	Climate	Age of wearer	Male or female?	Special purpose	Other things about this shoe

Getting Along

**"Do unto others as you wish others to do unto you.
Lucky numbers 22, 29, 37, 39, 45, 47."**

Fortune cookie

Each of us is one of many cookies in the great big cookie jar of life. To get along, we need to discover what goes into good relationships with others: respect, appreciation, courtesy, cooperation, and sharing. You'll explore those ideas in this theme, and learn a little bit about Chinese culture along the way.

The Yin and Yang of Respect

copies of handout on page 49

A traditional Chinese belief is that there are two great natural forces in the world, *yin* and *yang*. These forces stand for pairs of things that are opposites (examples: female/male, dark/light, and quiet/noise). For people to be healthy and get along, yin and yang need to balance harmoniously. On the handout, look at the Chinese symbol and think about how respect is related to harmony and balance. Below the symbol, write a definition of *respect*. When you're done, compare definitions with others in the class.

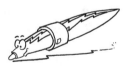

Daily Maxims

small slips of paper (fortune-cookie size) • small film canisters (free at photo shops) • shoe box to hold the canisters

A *maxim* is a short saying that gives wise advice. In the 1920s, a chef in San Francisco invented fortune cookies as a way of showing restaurant diners that maxims were a part of Chinese culture. On a small slip of paper, write a maxim that tells a way to get along with others. Put your maxim in a film canister (your variation on a fortune cookie) and place it in a shoe box with everyone else's. Mix up

the canisters. Then take one, open it, and read the maxim. (If you draw your own, return it to the box and choose another.) Keep the maxim with you all day, and try to do what it says. If you want, return the maxims to the box tomorrow and draw again. Keep drawing daily maxims and following their wise words.

Tai Chi Chuan

copies of handouts on page 50–51

Many Chinese people begin the day with exercises called *tai chi chuan*. They perform movements that help balance the needs of the mind, the body, and nature. The regular practice of tai chi chuan improves breathing, coordination, and blood pressure. It also reduces stress, emphasizes relaxation, and can be a form of self-defense. Try the two movements described on the handout.

Chinese Zodiac

copies of handouts on page 52–53

Look for the year of your birth on the Chinese zodiac. What a lucky number that is! The Chinese zodiac is based on a twelve-year cycle, with a different animal representing each year. Read what the year of your birth has to say about you. Then get together with others who share the same birth year. Discuss the traits mentioned. Do they fit in every case? Talk about how you can use your best traits to make the world a place where people get along together.

Character Drawing

copies of handout on page 54 • brushes • ink or paints

Written Chinese uses carefully drawn *characters* to express ideas. Look at the characters on the handout. Notice how the ancient characters looked like the objects they depicted. Then design and draw your own character representing what the Chinese scholar Confucius would call "the honorable good deed of sharing." When you're done drawing, bow respectfully to your teacher and classmates. Admire and compare all the different characters that can communicate a message of sharing.

Think About It, Talk About It

- Do you think all people deserve respect? Why or why not?

- Is courtesy important to you? Why or why not? Do you feel different when someone treats you courteously than when someone is rude?

- What are some times when it's hard to get along with others? What are some things you could do at school, at home, or with friends to help you and others get along?

- What are some ways people from different places or different groups might have trouble getting along? What can they do to get along better?

Affirmation

I can learn to get along with people who are different from me.

Resources

For Students

Schomp, Virginia. *The Ancient Chinese* (Franklin Watts, 2005). Learn the culture of a civilization that goes back 5,000 years. Part of the "People of the Ancient World" series.

For Teachers

Kuo, Simmone. *Long Life, Good Health through Tai-Chi Chuan* (North Atlantic Books, 1991). Step-by-step instructions and photographs help introduce a fascinating Chinese practice. Also includes the history and philosophy of this form of movement.

Yin and Yang

Yin and yang make up the Chinese symbol for balance and harmony. Look up the words *balance* and *harmony* in a dictionary. What does respect have to do with these ideas? Think about it, then write your own definition of *respect*.

Respect is

_____

_____

_____

_____

_____

_____

Tai Chi Chuan

As you try these tai chi chuan movements, keep in mind a few guidelines:

- Work for correct positions.
- Focus your mind on the exercises.
- Keep your fingers straight and palms flat.
- Breathe naturally and move smoothly.

First Movement

1

1. Stand straight with your feet together and your hands at your sides.
2. Turn your right foot slightly to the right, bend your knees, and extend your left foot forward so your left knee is straight, with your heel to the ground and your toes pointing up.
3. Keep your feet in position and raise your arms straight out so they are shoulder level. Turn your palms to the front.
4. Bring your hands together so they are almost touching, forming a shoulder-high circle with your arms.
5. With your hands still open, bend your right hand at the wrist so that it forms a right angle with the middle of your left hand. Hold this position and go on to the second movement.

5

2

3

4

Second Movement

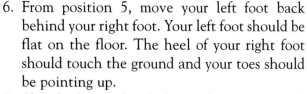

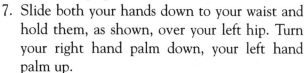

6. From position 5, move your left foot back behind your right foot. Your left foot should be flat on the floor. The heel of your right foot should touch the ground and your toes should be pointing up.

7. Slide both your hands down to your waist and hold them, as shown, over your left hip. Turn your right hand palm down, your left hand palm up.

8. Move your right leg back so your right foot is slightly raised and touches your left foot.

9. Step forward diagonally with your right foot. Bend both knees. Keeping your hands and palms as in position 7, raise your arms at the elbow as shown below. Your back should be straight.

10. Raise your arms and hands so they are shoulder height. Press your hands out at an angle. The angle of your right hand should match that of your right foot. Twist your shoulders and waist to make your hands even.

6

10

7

9

8

These ten positions are the first two movements of tai chi chuan. It has 78 movements in all. If you'd like to learn more, check your library or bookstore for the book *Long Life, Good Health through Tai-Chi Chuan* by Simmone Kuo.

Chinese Zodiac

Rat

Imaginative, charming, and generous, you're also willing to take advantage of opportunities that come your way. You may choose a career in sales or writing.

Ox

You are a born leader who likes hands-on work and takes things one step at a time. You have a tendency to want to have things your own way. Your future may hold a career as a military general, surgeon, or hairstylist.

Tiger

You can be sensitive and loving as well as stubborn. There may be a bit of the rebel in you as well. A career as a race-car driver, boss, or matador may be in store.

Rabbit

People like you because you're friendly and helpful. Take care not to be too willing to please. The role of an actor, a lawyer, or an ambassador may be in your future.

Dragon

An intelligent perfectionist who's full of enthusiasm, you also have a tendency to speak before thinking. This doesn't stop you from being well liked. Consider a career as an artist, a politician, or a religious leader.

Snake

Wisdom, charm, and a great sense of humor are the traits others admire in you. Your tendency to be thrifty could work for or against you. If you're thinking of being a teacher or psychiatrist, you're probably on the right track.

1948 1960 1972 1984 1996 2008

1949 1961 1973 1985 1997 2009

1950 1962 1974 1986 1998 2010

1951 1963 1975 1987 1999 2011

1952 1964 1976 1988 2000 2012

1953 1965 1977 1989 2001 2013

Pig

Open-minded, honest, and sincere, you are also able to set difficult goals for yourself and meet them. It can be hard for you not to expect these same traits in others. Guard against placing too high a value on material things. Your future may find you entertaining stage or screen audiences or arguing as a lawyer in the courtroom.

Dog

You're a friend through thick and thin, someone people know they can trust to keep their secrets. Watch your tongue, though, and try to worry a bit less. Consider a career as an activist, a teacher, or a secret agent.

Rooster

You're a hard worker and a dreamer— and a flashy dresser! Be aware that others sometimes mistake your confidence for boastfulness. Some day you may travel the world, own a restaurant, or serve as a soldier for your country.

Monkey

You are smart, clever, and well liked. Strive to be more trustful of others, and you can be successful in any career you may choose.

Goat

You possess great charm and are known for your sense of artistry. You might want to make an effort to be more optimistic. The future may find you working on the stage or in a garden.

Horse

You are truly your own person—independent, intelligent, and hard-working. You'll do well to fall back on your friendly nature rather than letting yourself become too self-centered. Life as an adventurer, a scientist, or a poet could be in your future.

Years on wheel: 1959 1971 1983 1995 2007 2019; 1958 1970 1982 1994 2006 2018; 1957 1969 1981 1993 2005 2017; 1956 1968 1980 1992 2004 2016; 1955 1967 1979 1991 2003 2015; 1954 1966 1978 1990 2002 2014

Word Characters

Written Chinese uses carefully drawn characters to express ideas. Look at the characters below. They are shown in both the ancient and the modern Chinese styles.

Ancient Chinese	Modern Chinese
sun	sun
bird	bird
sheep	sheep
water	water
tree	tree

Design and draw your own character here:

Teamwork

"Snowflakes are one of nature's most fragile things, but just look what they can do when they stick together."

Verna M. Kelly, in Hillary Rodham Clinton's *It Takes a Village*

Teamwork is the effort of working together for a common goal. If we look to our immediate world—to our school, community, or family—we'll see teamwork all around us. It's not always easy to get along as a team. Let's learn a few of the principles of teamwork through some games and art projects.

Note: Do the second and third "Teamwork" activities in sequence.

 ## Coloring Book

heavy drawing paper • pencils • black fine-line markers • stapler • construction paper for the book's cover (optional)

Tip: Before stapling, photocopy the pages to make several books.

Team up to make a coloring book for younger kids. As a class, choose a subject for the coloring book (examples: animals, dinosaurs, or toys). Work with a partner. Fold the drawing paper in half. With the folded edge to the left, draw a picture for a child to color. Keep your picture simple, with lots of space for coloring. Sketch with a pencil, then go over the outline with a black fine-line marker. Open the drawing paper and draw a second picture on the inside-right page. Combine all the folded pages. If you want, make a construction-paper cover for the book, too. Staple the sheets together on the fold.

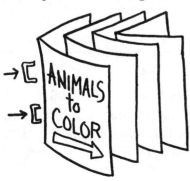

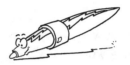 ## Game Plans

books or other sources with a variety of game ideas (optional—see "Resources," page 57)

Team up with a few classmates. Agree on a game you all like to play. Make it something you could play right in the classroom. Together, make a list of the materials needed and write clear directions for playing the game. Post the game plans and save them for one more activity.

 ## Playing Games

game plans from the preceding activity • materials needed to play the games

Look at the various game plans you and your class-mates have written. Form teams, choose a game, and play it. Are the directions clear? Would you like to change the rules? Go ahead—as long as everyone on your team agrees. Enjoy the games and the team spirit that goes with them!

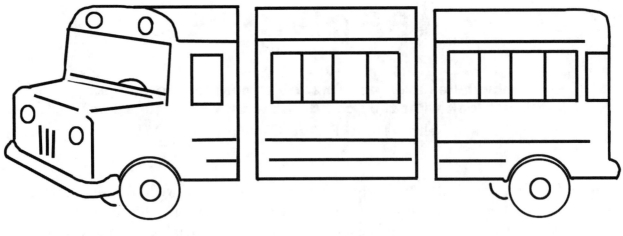

 **Bus Puzzles**

drawing paper • pencils • markers • tape

Teacher: For younger children, draw bus segments on sheets of drawing paper as shown above. Older students can draw the outlines for themselves. *Students:* Team up with two other people to form a group of three. Look at your team's three sheets of drawing paper. Each sheet is part of a school bus. Your team's goal is to turn the sections into a complete bus filled with kids on their way to school. Decide how you'll finish the pages. Will you sketch with pencil first, or start right in with markers? Will you use one color, or many? Finish the parts of the school bus and tape them together. Look at all the school buses together. How are they alike? How are they different? How did each team decide on a way to illustrate their bus parts?

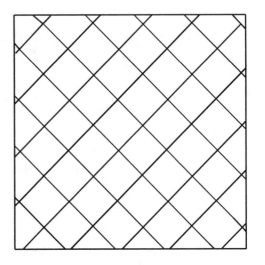

 **Class "Quilt"**

9" x 9" squares of construction paper in your school colors • markers in your school colors

Have you ever looked closely at a patchwork quilt? Each square is a small work of art in itself. Together, the squares form patterns that can be bright or soft, simple or detailed. Individually, make squares for a quilt. Use your school colors.

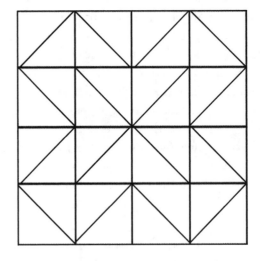

Draw a pattern you've seen, or make up your own. When everyone's finished, pin the squares to the bulletin board to form a quilt. Stand back and admire how your patterns fit together!

Think About It, Talk About It

- Is it easy to plan and carry out games and projects as a team? Why or why not?

- What were some problems you had working together as a team? How did you solve them?

- How is working or playing as a team different from doing so on your own?

Affirmation

I can be a team player by working together with others for a common goal.

Resources

For Students

Holohan, Maureen. *Friday Nights* (Aladdin, 2001). For a group of young teenage girls, what starts out as playing sports for fun turns into serious teamwork in a tough summer basketball league. Ages 10 and up.

My Best Friend

"My best friend is the one who brings out the best in me."
Henry Ford (1863–1947), U.S. automobile engineer and manufacturer

A best friend is one of the best things to have in the world. How do we form a "best" friend-ship? How do we get along when the road gets rocky? Let's explore some of the ups and downs of having—or finding—a best friend.

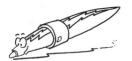

Secret Message

permanent ink pens • pencils

You can share special things with a close friend. Using a pen, write a special message to your best friend. After completing the message, take a lead pencil and cover the message so no one can read it. Pass the message along to your best friend with instructions to erase the pencil carefully to reveal a special message meant just for that friend.

Advice Letters

copies of handout on page 60

Many newspapers have a column called "Dear Abby." People write to Abby about their prob-lems, and she writes answers that are printed in the newspaper. Imagine that you write an advice column. Look at the handout. Put your own name on the blank line at the top. Read the letter. Then write an answer giving your best advice for finding and making a best friend. Have volunteers read their advice out loud. If you hear some good advice, try it out!

Problem-Solving Role-Plays

Even the best of friends sometimes disagree. As a large group, talk about some problems friends can have getting along. One problem at a time, share ideas for working out the problems. Role-play a way to solve each problem.

Friendship Portraits

copies of handout on page 61 • drawing pencils, colored pencils, or markers

You might have a photograph of your best friend already. Here's your chance to draw a portrait of this friend as you see him or her. Look at the picture frame handout. Inside the frame, draw a picture of your best friend or the ideal friend you'd like to have. Decorate the frame in a way that suits your friend. Keep this picture for your wall at home, or give it to your friend to keep.

"High Five" Pop-up Greetings

9" x 12" construction paper • markers • pencils • scissors • tagboard cut in 1" x 4" strips • glue

Make a greeting card for your best friend or for someone you'd like to get to know. Fold a piece of construction paper in half. On the front, write your friend's name. If you like, add a few words of greeting. On a second sheet of construction paper, trace your hand and cut it out. Fold strips of tagboard accordion style. Glue one folded end to the back of your hand cutout, others to the back of some or all of the fingers. Open the card and glue the other ends of the folded strips in the center of the right-hand inside of the card. If you like, add some friendly words or pictures to your pop-up hand. Close the card and open it. Do you see the "high five"? Give this "high five" greeting to your friend!

Think About It, Talk About It

- What are some ways to find and make a best friend?

- Do you think it's possible to have more than one best friend? Why?

- What are the qualities that make a best friend?

- What are some things that help friends get along and grow in their friendship?

- When you and your best friend don't get along, what do you do about it?

Affirmation

I can form bonds with a special friend.

Resources

For Students

Lowry, Lois. *Number the Stars* (Laurel Leaf, 1998). Annemarie and her best friend, Ellen, play like other ten-year-olds until the Nazis terrorize the Jews of Denmark in 1943. Annemarie must be brave and save her friend's life. A 1990 Newbery Medal winner. Ages 9–12.

Pomerantz, Charlotte, illustrations by David Soman. *You're Not My Best Friend Anymore* (Dial Books for Young Readers, 1998). Best friends Molly and Ben live in a two-family house and do everything together. When a big disagreement splits them apart, they find a way to resolve their differences. Ages 8–10.

Rockett's New School (Purple Moon, 1997). This CD-ROM software offers girls opportunities to think through issues of friendship. They learn that different characteristics, such as a sense of humor, popularity, and kindness, mold a relationship. Ages 8–12.

Advice Letter

Dear _____ :

I've been looking for a best friend for a long time.
I just can't seem to find one. Can you give me some
advice about how I can make and keep a best friend?

Yours truly,

A Friend in Waiting

Dear Friend in Waiting:

Friendship Portrait

Helping Each Other

"If you want happiness for a lifetime, help someone else."
Chinese proverb

As our awareness and understanding of friends, family, and classmates grow, we begin to see ways that we can help each other. Every day offers many opportunities for us to do this. Let's lend a helping hand!

Heart Coupons

copies of handout on page 64 • colored pencils or markers • scissors

Tip: Make extra copies of the handout for students who want to make more than one coupon.

Could someone you care about use your help? Think of a gift of help you could offer someone. Could a parent use a night off from kitchen cleanup? Would younger sisters or brothers like you to teach them to tie their shoes or ride a bike? Could a friend use a study buddy? Look at the sample coupons on the handout. Then fill in the large coupon with words or pictures to show your loved one what you promise to do. Cut it out and present it. Enjoy giving help from your heart.

Stories About Helping

a length of rope, twine, or ribbon (approx. 4')

Secure a length of rope, twine, or ribbon from the edge of the chalkboard or bulletin board. Take turns sharing stories or ideas related to helping or being helped. The stories might be about times you've helped a person or someone has helped you. Or, they might be ideas for reaching out to others in simple ways—by giving a cheery greeting, bringing someone a snack, or sharing with a classmate. As each story is told, tie a knot in the rope to create a "counting rope" of helping others. The knots are visible signs of the many ways you are helping each other.

Help Essay

Think of a time a friend helped you when you really needed it. Write a few sentences or a paragraph describing what you needed help with, how the friend helped, and why it was important to you.

Helping Role-Plays

Form small groups. One by one in your groups, talk about what kind of help you or someone else might need. Together, discuss ways people could help. Then role-play the situation.

Helping Hand

drawing paper • pencils • scissors • pens, colored pencils, or fine-line markers • string • tape

Make a helping hand for recording your acts of kindness. Trace your hand on a sheet of paper and cut it out. Think of one act of kindness you've done for someone. Write it in one of the fingers. Tie a small string around one paper finger. The string is a reminder that you can make a difference no matter what your age or size. Attach your paper hand to the inside of your desk, locker, or bedroom door. Over a week, keep your eyes and ears open for ways to assist others at home or at school. Record each act of kindness on your traced hand. Fill in each finger and the thumb, or fill in the whole hand.

Think About It, Talk About It

- Can kids help adults as much as adults can help kids? In what ways?

- How do you know when you need help? How can you ask for help when you need it?

- How do you know when someone else needs help? What are some ways to offer help?

- Do you think you could get along with no help from other people? Why or why not?

Affirmation

I will help my friends, my classmates, my teacher, and my family.

Resources

For Students

Martin, Bill, Jr., and John Archambault, illustrations by Ted Rand. *Knots on a Counting Rope* (Henry Holt & Co., Reprint, 1997). A Native American grandfather reaches out to help build his grandson's confidence through stories of how people, animals, and the natural world help and have helped the boy. Ages 4–8.

Stewart, Sarah, illustrations by David Small. *The Gardener* (Farrar, Straus & Giroux, 1997). Through small acts of kindness, Lydia Grace helps her grouchy uncle and creates a rooftop garden. Simply written and charmingly illustrated, this Caldecott Honor Book is suitable for readers of all ages.

Heart Coupons

Read the sample coupons. Then make your own coupon offering help to someone you care about.

I promise to help my little brother by walking to the bus with him instead of running ahead.

Julia Sanchez

Grandpa, I promise to help you pack lunches for school whenever you want me to.

Matt

Celebrating Differences

**"No matter what language we speak,
we all live under the same moon and stars."**
John Denver (1943–1997), U.S. singer and songwriter

Each of us is a distinct individual with our own particular family and background and our own unique likes, dislikes, abilities, and interests. Sharing the ways we're different expands the world for all of us. Let's discover and celebrate some of these differences.

TV Reports

Tip: Repeat this activity from time to time to hear about a variety of different families.

Get ready to dig up information and present it like the reporters you see on the TV news. Find a partner. Interview each other to learn about how your families are different. Who is in your partner's family? When did your partner's family or ancestors come to this country? Does the family have favorite foods, music, or pastimes? After you've learned something about each other, have a few volunteers give 20-second "news bulletins" about something they learned in the interview. Example:

This just in from our satellite service: Fifth grader Mattie Makimba told this reporter today that her father and grandmother came to the United States fifteen years ago from Kenya.

Kenya is a country in eastern Africa. Mattie's family speaks both English and Swahili, the official language of Kenya.

I asked Mattie to teach me a Swahili greeting. Here it is: Jambo.

Hoop Games

hula hoops • sticks for rolling hoops • balls

Tip: After trying the historic games, make up a few of your own.

People in many different parts of the world have played hoop games. Try one of these hoop games from a distant time and place.

Hoop rolling: The ancient Greeks and Romans got hoops rolling smoothly and rapidly, then tried to jump and run through them. In your classroom, you can play a variation of the game by having someone hold the hoop higher and higher for you to jump through.

Tossing a ball through a hoop: The Aztecs and Mayas of Mexico played a game with a rubber ball and a stone ring. Try your own version of this game by trying to roll a lightweight ball through a hoop held upright on the floor. Use your elbows or knees—no hands or feet allowed!

Differences Are Good Because . . .

As a class, make a list of 30 reasons it's good to be different. Be creative, and have fun!

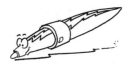

Where I'd Like to Go

CD or tape player with international music (optional)

Tip: Set a mood by playing music from different parts of the world.

Write a paragraph about a place in the world you'd like to visit. Tell why you want to go there and how you think that place is different from where you live now. What will you find there? What will you do? How will it be different from where you live now?

Paper Bag Hats

copies of handout on page 67 • medium-sized brown or white paper bags • scissors • construction paper • glue or tape • other decorative materials (optional)

Throughout history, people have used hats for many different purposes. Look at the variety of hats on the handout. Who might wear each hat? What might each hat be used for? Notice the things many hats have in common: a crown, a brim, and a band. Now it's your turn to create your own personal hat. Start with a paper bag. Plan a brim or a band for it—or both. Have fun creating a unique hat that's just right for you.

Think About It, Talk About It

- What activities do you think you have in common with kids from other parts of the country? Of the world?

- Do you think family life, play, and school are different in different parts of the world? In what ways?

- Are differences among people good or bad? Explain your answer.

- Why do you think people are different from each other?

Affirmation

By accepting and respecting others, I celebrate the many differences that make up this planet.

Resources

For Students

A Child's Celebration of the World (Music for Little People, Warner Brothers Records, 1998). Listen and enjoy multicultural music sung in various languages by artists around the world. The music will be enjoyed by older as well as younger kids. Find the cassette or CD in your local children's book or toy store, or write to Music for Little People, P.O. Box 1460, Redway, CA 95560-1460. Toll-free phone: 1-800-409-2457. Web site: www.musicforlittlepeople.com

Steele, Philip. *The Kingfisher Young People's Atlas of the World* (Kingfisher, 1997). A perfect introduction to lands, people, and customs around the world. Ages 9–12.

Hats, Hats, Hats

Helping Others

"Children must be involved in finding solutions to the problems facing them."

Craig Kielburger, founder at age 12 of the international youth organization Free the Children

We all need help at times, and we all need to give help. In finding ways to help others, we serve as agents of goodwill—for our school, our community, our nation, and our world. Where problems exist, we can become part of the solution. Knowing that there are solutions to problems—and that we can help solve them—boosts our confidence and sense of self-worth. Let's look some more at ways we can help others and they can help us.

Note: Do the first three "Helping Others" activities in sequence.

Honoring Local "Stars"

copies of handout on page 70 • yellow construction paper • scissors • colored pencils or markers • hole punch • thread or string

Sometimes you don't have to look to the heavens or far from home to find a shining star. Make a list of everyday people who help within your school or community—local "stars" such as police officers, mail carriers, pharmacists, shop owners, and librarians. Discuss how their roles improve the lives of you and your family. Cut out large stars and draw community helpers. Punch holes at the top, attach string, and hang the stars from the ceiling. Let their bright light shine!

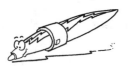

"Star" Letters

stationery and envelopes • stamps

Write short letters to the local "stars" you honored in the last activity. Explain how you selected them and why you believe their help deserves recognition. Invite these people to your classroom to view the art you've created in their honor.

Newspaper "Stars"

As a class, write a short article for your school newspaper listing people who help within your school or community. You may want to tell about the artistic tribute you've made to these helpers.

The "Do's" of Helping Others

construction paper or posterboard • markers • tape

You've seen lists of "Do's and Don'ts." Get rid of the negative and emphasize the positive by organizing a "Do's of Helping Others Day." Post simple notices around the room or the halls. Then jump into action. *Do* open doors for teachers and guests. *Do* wait your turn in line or on the stairs. *Do* offer compliments, praise, and thanks to friends. What other "do's" can you think of?

Service Project Talks

Tip: Have a speaker talk to your group about a local service project that could use help from kids.

People and organizations often give money to fund programs working to help others. What are some ways this money helps? How can kids help an important cause without spending money? As a group, talk about ways to get involved in service projects in the local or global community. Do any ideas interest you? Check the local paper, the library, or the Internet for ideas.

Think About It, Talk About It

- What would community life be like if we didn't have doctors? Garbage collectors? Politicians? What other important helpers can you think of?

- At school, how can helping in small ways make school better for everyone?

- Do you think children can really make a difference in solving big world problems? Why or why not?

Affirmation

I can help others and make a difference.

Resources

For Students

Free the Children. Founded by a twelve-year-old, this organization works to aid exploited children throughout the world. Contact the organization to learn about ways you can become involved. Write to Free the Children U.S.A., P.O. Box 32099, Hartford, CT 06150-2099. Telephone: (416) 925-5894. Web site: www.freethechildren.org

Lewis, Barbara A. *The Kid's Guide to Service Projects: Over 500 Service Ideas for Young People Who Want to Make a Difference* (Free Spirit Publishing, 1998). This book guides kids through small-to-large commitments including animals, crime fighting, the environment, friendship, hunger, literacy, and transportation. Also includes a section with instructions for creating fliers, petitions, and more. Ages 10 and up.

For Teachers

Springer, Jane. *Listen to Us: The World's Working Children* (Groundwood Books, 1998). The author, who worked with UNICEF and other agencies to better the lives of child workers, wrote this book to increase concern about child labor worldwide. The book contains some harsh stories of children's lives and is suitable for sharing with older children. Ages 9–12.

Star Template

Making Peace

"Peace begins with you."
Katherine Scholes, U.S. author

It's impossible not to be aware of the violence that exists in our world. Yet each of us can choose to live peacefully together, and can work to help others make that choice as well. Accepting differences, respecting others, and learning to listen and compromise give us the tools we need. By putting our heads together, we can discover ways to make peace.

Note: Do the first two "Making Peace" activities in sequence.

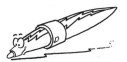

Problem-Solving Plan

Think of a time when you've had an argument or a fight. It might have been at home or at school. What happened? Think of a peaceful way you could handle that problem in the future. Write about your problem-solving plan. If you want, share your plan with others in the class. Who else has ideas for solving the conflict peacefully? Save what you've written for the next activity.

Solution Drawing

problem-solving plans from preceding activity • drawing paper • colored pencils or markers in soft colors

Review your problem-solving plan. Now illustrate your peaceful, positive solution. Use soft colors to give your picture a gentle mood.

Peace Plays

Quickly think of four or five conflicts that happen in school. Write them on the board. Then form small groups. In your group, choose one of the conflicts and agree on a way to solve it peacefully. Briefly act out the conflict and the peacemaking solution. Do your groups deserve the Nobel Peace Prize for their peaceful solutions?

Peace Signs

copies of handout on page 73

Have you ever made a New Year's resolution? In small groups, think of four peaceful world resolutions. The shape on the handout is a peace sign. Write your resolutions in the four sections of the peace sign. Share them with the rest of the class. After class, keep your resolutions in mind. Practice peacemaking wherever you go!

Peace Dance

Some dances express people's desire to get along peacefully. Learn a simple Native American toe-heel dance—a traditional dance used at the beginning of a powwow. As the performers enter the dancing area, they come in peace to celebrate and share their heritage with visiting tribes.

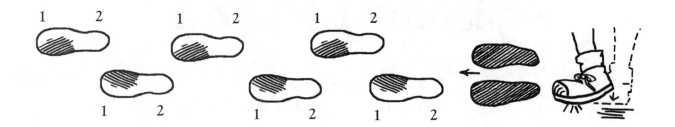

Stand beside your desk. Starting with your left foot, touch the ground lightly with your toe, then bring your heel down hard. Repeat with the right foot. Alternate feet. Go forward with your group. Go side to side. Go backward. Use your hands to make drumbeats on your desk as you dance. Dance away your conflicts and make peace with those around you!

Think About It, Talk About It

- Why can it be hard to solve conflicts between friends or brothers and sisters peacefully? What are some ways to make this easier?

- Why do you think it's sometimes hard for one group of people to make peace with another? Give examples. What agreements must people make to have a positive and peaceful resolution?

- What do you think children can do to help bring about a more peaceful world?

Affirmation

Making peace through positive and peaceful problem solving leads to a better world.

Resources

For Students

Scholes, Katherine, illustrations by Robert Ingpen. *Peace Begins with You* (Sierra Club Books/Little, Brown & Co., Reissue ed. 1994). Clearly and simply explains to children how and why peace is important in all our lives. The author explores the many ways conflicts can be resolved at home and around the globe. Ages 4–8.

For Teachers

Baskwill, Jane, illustrations by Stephanie Carter. *If Peace Is . . .* (Mondo Publishing, 2003). Colorful illustrations and simple, rhyming text describe peace. Ages 4–8.

Peace Corps, Coverdell World Wise Schools. Contribute to the Peace Corps' Gifts in Kind Program, correspond with a volunteer, receive global education lesson plans, and find speakers for your classroom. Write to Peace Corps, Coverdell World Wise Schools, 1111 20th Street NW, Washington, DC 20526. Toll-free phone: 1-800-424-8580. Web site: www.peacecorps.gov/wws

Peace Sign

Succeeding in School

Managing My Time

"I must govern the clock, not be governed by it."

Golda Meir (1898–1978), Russian-born Israeli Prime Minister

Learning to manage your time is a skill that can help you throughout your life. Use these activities to look at how you spend your time, how you *want* to spend it, and how you can keep yourself from being too busy or not busy enough.

Note: Do the first two "Managing My Time" activities in sequence.

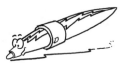

Weekly Calendar

copies of handout on page 78

Find out where your time goes during a whole week. Fill out the calendar on the handout. For each day, include everything you typically do on that day—from eating breakfast to going to school to watching TV before bedtime. Look at your schedule. Are you doing the things you want to do? Are you too busy? Not busy enough? Write some ideas for using your time in the way that's best for you. Remember, we all need time for both work and play. Save your calendar for one more activity.

Changes in the Calendar

calendars from preceding activity

In small groups, share your weekly calendars and talk about how you spend your time and how you could change your routine for the better. Do you need to figure out a regular time to do homework? Do you want more time for a sport or hobby? Help each person in your group think of a way to make a needed change.

Time Promise

copies of handout on page 79 • colored pencils or markers • tape

Is there something you've been wishing you had time to do? On the handout, write a promise to yourself about one thing you will make time to do today or in the next few days. Draw a picture that shows you doing this activity. Tape your promise inside your desk or locker, or to a mirror at home. Keep your promise!

Yoga Time

copies of handout on page 80

Taking a few minutes each day to stretch your muscles and center your mind is time well spent. One great way to do this is with *yoga*. Yoga was first developed in ancient India. It helps balance the body and mind in a way that makes you stronger and sharpens your mind, memory, and concentration. Try the yoga movements on the handout. Feel your mind and body coming into balance.

Time Without a Clock

Think about all the gadgets in your life that keep you "on time." Now imagine a day without clocks, bells, or alarms. How would you get through your day without these timekeepers? How would you know when to get up? Go to school? Eat? Would you spend your time differently? What would you like about not having a clock? What wouldn't you like? If you want, set aside a day for going without a clock. Report back to your classmates on what your "timeless" day was like.

Think About It, Talk About It

- Do you think most people use their time wisely? Why or why not?

- What do you think is the most important thing to spend time on? Why?

- Do you wish a grown-up in your family would spend more time with you? How could you let that person know you'd like some time together?

Affirmation

I can plan ways to spend time doing what's important to me.

Resources

For Students

Ash, Russell. *The World in One Day* (DK Publishing, 1997). Describes the amazing things that happen in a typical day's time, such as the earth's geological changes, the production of the world's goods, and what people do on their days off. Ages 9–12.

Lark, Liz. *Yoga for Kids* (Firefly Books, 2003). Step-by-step photos demonstrate basic yoga poses to help kids maintain good posture, flexible joints, and firm muscles.

Weekly Calendar

Fill in the seven calendar spaces with all the things you do. Include home, school, and outside activities as well as what you do when you're just "hanging around."

Monday	Tuesday	Wednesday	Thursday	Friday	Saturday	Sunday

I think I'm doing: _____ too much _____ too little _____ just the right amount

Here's what I'd like to change:

Here's how I could change it:

Time Promise

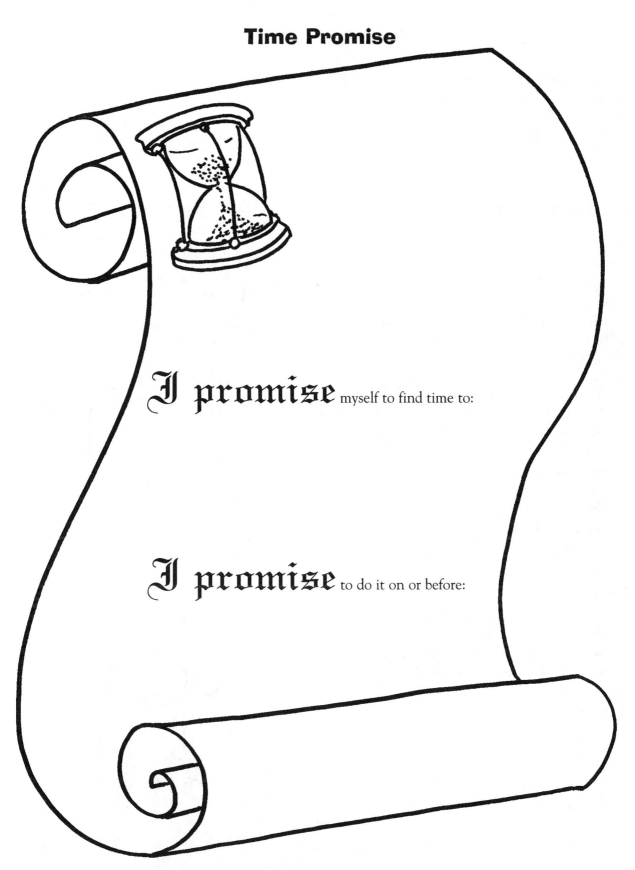

$\mathfrak{I}$ **promise** myself to find time to:

$\mathfrak{I}$ **promise** to do it on or before:

Yoga Movements

As you try these yoga movements, keep in mind a few guidelines:
- Never compete in yoga.
- Be relaxed.
- Breathe deeply.
- Don't strain.
- End each exercise by resting completely while you count to ten.

One-Leg Stretch

1. Stand on your left leg. Bend your right leg and pull your right foot up to your left thigh. Grip your right ankle with both hands.
2. Keep your foot pressed against your thigh. Breathe in and slowly raise your arms above your head with your fingertips touching. Hold for ten counts.
3. Repeat with the opposite leg.

1

2

3

Arching

1. Kneel with your legs slightly apart.
2. Breathe in as you bend back, arching your back. Grasp your ankles and relax your neck. Hold for ten counts while you breathe normally.
3. Repeat five times.

2

Making a List

"In life, all of us can make two lists. The first list is things you can do something about. The second list is things you can't change. How tall you are, you can't do anything about it. So that's it."

Michael J. Fox, Canadian-born actor

Whether you make lists for fun or for getting things done, they can help you put some order in your life. Here are some activities to get you started. Sharpen your pencil and let's begin.

"Things I'm Glad I Can't Change" List

Read the quote by Michael J. Fox. Now think about some things in your life you can't change. Go one step further: think of things you can't change but you're happy about anyway, just as they are. Make a list of the things you're glad you can't change. Keep your list and add to it.

Things I'm Glad I Can't Change

that I'm a twin

that I can sing

that we don't have to move after all

that I can finally really hit! (when the pitch is a good one)

Priority Picture

drawing paper • colored pencils or markers

Take a few minutes to list a dozen things you do in a day's time. Start with waking up, eating breakfast, and so on, until you've gotten to bed in the evening. What are the two or three most enjoyable or important things you do? Circle them. Out of the things circled, choose one favorite activity. Illustrate it. It's a daily gift you give to yourself. Enjoy it!

Athletic Moves

In teams of three or four, talk about some of your favorite athletes. What sport does each athlete play? With your team, list at least two physical skills or movements needed for each sport (examples: arm strokes and leg kicks for swimming, jumping and dunking for basketball). Do the moves together. Notice the variety of sport moves the other groups have come up with, too.

Almanacs

drawing paper • colored pencils, markers, or fine-line markers • sample almanacs (optional)

An *almanac* is a book of lists, charts, and tables of information about one thing or many unrelated things. Think about a friend or family member. What is one of this person's special interests? Make an almanac sheet for that person by drawing and writing information about the person's interest. For example, for someone who loves music you could list ten favorite songs, draw a picture or diagram of a guitar, and write the person's favorite song lyrics. Give the almanac sheet to that special person.

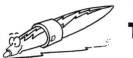

TGIF

"TGIF" stands for "Thank Goodness It's Friday." By the week's end, you're ready for a change. Make your own TGIF list. It might tell all the reasons you're glad it's Friday, or some of the activities you're looking forward to doing on the weekend. When you're done, take a few minutes for volunteers to share some of the things on their list that make them say "TGIF!"

Think About It, Talk About It

- Do you think writing a list is worth the time it takes to do so? Explain your views.

- Imagine that each day this week you've made a daily "to-do" list. No matter how hard you try, you can't seem to get everything on the list done. What might be the problem? What can you do about it?

- Can you think of jobs where making lists is important? Name them. What are some things that might be on the lists?

Affirmation

Making a list can help me be more organized and choose what's most important to me.

Resources

For Students

Ash, Russell. *Top 10 of Everything: 2006* (DK Publishing, 2005). This book contains more than 900 lists of facts and trivia on toys, sports, music, culture, learning, and more. All ages.

Choron, Sandra, and Harry Choron. *The All-New Book of Lists for Kids* (Houghton Mifflin, 2002). A fun-filled book of over three hundred lists that will get kids thinking and giggling, such as 20 kinds of marbles, 60 good deeds, and 8 new colors of Crayola Crayons. Ages 9–12.

Planning Ahead

"When you have a great and difficult task, something perhaps almost impossible, if you only work a little at a time, every day a little, suddenly the work will finish itself."

Isak Dinesen (1885–1962), Danish writer

Planning ahead gives you control over the things you enjoy and the things you find hard to do. Don't just wait for things to happen. Take charge of your school and personal life with some thoughtful planning.

Plan for a Long-Term Assignment

copies of handout on page 85

Think about a long-term assignment you have. It may be a science project, a report, or a paper. Imagine the assignment as a long road ahead. You can plan the destinations along the way and how to reach each one. On the handout, fill in the billboards with the steps you'll follow to complete your assignment successfully.

Plan for a Tough Subject

Many people have at least one subject in school that's harder for them than others. Do you struggle when it comes to writing a book report? Worry when there's a test? Do your eyes glaze over when you have math word problems? Find a partner. Talk to each other about what school subject or type of work is most difficult for each of you. Together, come up with some strategies for getting help. Be willing to listen and consider new ideas.

Plan for Dealing with Distractions

drawing paper • colored pencils or markers

When it comes to studying, what distracts you? Is it the sound of kids playing outside? The lure of the television? Phone calls that interrupt? As a class, talk for a few minutes about some ways to overcome distractions at study time. Write down ideas that might work for you. Then draw a picture of yourself following one of the ideas to keep studying when other things could be distracting you. Display your picture in the place where you study as a reminder that you can concentrate on getting the job done.

Personal Plan

Besides school, other parts of your life need your thought and planning. Think of an activity away from school that you currently do or would like to do. Why is it important to you? Is it a skill you want to build? Do you need the help of a friend or a grown-up to help you enjoy or improve at the activity? Write a few sentences telling how you plan to proceed with your chosen activity in the months ahead. Keep your plan private or share it—that's up to you.

Future Plans

What do you see yourself doing in the future? In small groups, talk about things each of you can plan and begin to do now so you can someday reach that goal. For example, if you want to be a stockbroker, you'll need to plan ways to learn how the stock market works and how to invest successfully. To do this, you might use the business section of the newspaper or the Internet. You might find games that will help you learn about how the stock market works. What ideas can your classmates offer to help you plan for your goal? What ideas can you offer them for theirs?

Think About It, Talk About It

- How can planning ahead help you in school? In other parts of your life?

- Is it ever possible to do too much planning? Explain your answer.

- Think of someone you admire who is doing something similar to what you hope to do someday. How has watching that person made you want to pursue your plan? Why do you admire the person?

Affirmation

By planning ahead,
I can accomplish my goals.

Resources

For Students

Fly Away Home (Columbia Tri-Star, 1997). Adapted from a true story, this movie tells how a thirteen-year-old girl and her father devise a plan to care for orphaned geese and take part in the geese's natural flight south to warm weather. Rated PG.

Manes, Stephen. *Be a Perfect Person in Just Three Days* (Yearling Books, 1996). In this hilarious tale, Milo plans to follow an instruction book to become a perfect person. He learns a lot about himself, including that being perfect may not be what he really wants. Ages 9–12.

The Road to Success

Write the steps you'll follow to complete a long-term assignment successfully.

My Recipe for School Success

"Even if you're on the right track, you'll get run over if you just sit there."

Will Rogers (1879–1935), U.S. cowboy philosopher and comedian

You know that school is the right track to be on. There's more to getting the most out of school than just being there, though. Take time to discover some of the ingredients that will give you your own recipe for school success.

 ## "Helps and Hinders" Lists

chart paper and marker • tape

Write two column headings on chart paper: "Helps" and "Hinders." Talk about the things that *help* you to succeed in school. Write each helpful thing under the "Helps" column. Also talk about things that *hinder* you from doing well—things that get in the way or actually hurt your chances of success. Work together to compile a list. Leave the list taped to the board or the wall as a reminder for starting each school day with the right attitude.

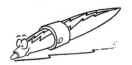 ## Recipes

recipe cards

Talk briefly about things that distract you when you are trying to study. (You might refer back to the "Plan for Dealing with Distractions" activity on page 83.) Then write a "recipe" that tells what to do to overcome a distraction.

Recipe for Studying on a Warm Spring Day

Close shades.

Turn on light.

Imagine that it's raining outside.

When done studying, treat yourself

to a little time outdoors.

 ## Exercise Break

radio or CD or tape player with favorite music for movement (optional)

Exercise is an important ingredient in any recipe for school success. Exercise refreshes and strengthens your body *and* your mind. As a group, take ten minutes to do a simple exercise routine. Turn on some music if you like. Then:

- Stand up. Put your hands above your head and do long, slow windmill stretches from side to side. Do 25 stretches on each side.

- Place your hands on your hips. Keeping your feet solidly on the floor, slowly turn your trunk to the left and then to the right. Do 25 twists.
- Balance on your right leg and count to ten. Then balance on your left. Repeat four times on each leg.
- Sit at your desk. Raise your left leg in front of you and point the toe out, then pull your toes upward to stretch the back of your calf. Rotate (turn) your left foot. Repeat with your right leg.
- Keeping your feet flat on the floor, shake out your hands at the wrists. Stretch all ten fingers and release them several times.
- Tilt your head to the right and then the left, gently and slowly stretching the neck muscles.
- Breathe deep and hold your breath for a count of five. Breathe out. Repeat five times.

Certificate of Success

copies of handout on page 88

As you work toward more school success, remember that successes can be both big and small. Have you recently received a good grade? Improved in a subject? Helped with a project? Cheered a classmate on? Recognize the success you've already had! Fill in and decorate the "Certificate of Success." Have a teacher or classmate sign it, or sign it yourself. Take the certificate home and share it with your family. Let it spur you on to further success.

Thank-You Notes

stationery or other writing paper

Your school success depends on others, too. Who helps you succeed at school? Is it a teacher? A classmate? A parent? A sister or brother? A friend? Give that special person something in return by writing a thank-you note straight from your heart. Compliment the person's work, talent, and efforts. Make someone's day!

Think About It, Talk About It

- Why is it important to have success in school?

- Do you feel better physically and mentally when you've had a successful school day? Why?

- Read the Will Rogers quote at the top of page 86. What does the quote say about the way to succeed in school?

Affirmation

To succeed in school, my attitude
is an important ingredient. I can create
a recipe for success!

Resources

For Teachers

Faber, Adele, and Elaine Mazlish. *How to Talk So Kids Can Learn at Home and in School* (Sound Ideas, 2005). This abridged audio CD is a guide to show parents and teachers how to motivate kids to learn and succeed.

Certificate of Success

This certifies that

_____

has been successful at

_____

_____

_____
Signature

_____
Date

Goodbye to Homework Hassles

"The work will teach you how to do it."
Estonian proverb

Do you wish homework would just disappear? There's no magic way to get rid of homework, but there are some "tricks" you can use to help take the hassles out of it. Who knows? You might even find yourself enjoying this daily task!

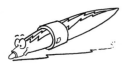

Homework Checklist

copies of handout on page 91

Would homework be easier if you had a fast, handy way to decide what books and materials to bring home? Make your own personal form to fill in and follow each day. First, fill in the handout with the subjects you have in school. Then make several copies of the form. Use one copy each week, listing everything you need to bring home and checking off each item before leaving school.

"Tricks" for Easier Homework

Sometimes the trick to succeeding at anything is to find an approach that works for you. Often you have to try different approaches before you succeed. Try this lifting "trick": Can two people lift one person? Form teams of three. First, have the person to be lifted stand straight, hands on shoulders, elbows pointed forward. With your other partner, try to gently lift the person by the elbows. Can you do it? Can you think of another way to pick the person up by the elbows? (The "trick" is to have the person's bent arms squeezed against the sides of the body with elbows pointing down.)

Talk together about how you approach your homework. Are there some "tricks" that might make homework go more smoothly? (Examples: studying after school or right after supper instead of just before bed; doing the hardest assignment first rather than last.)

Homework Plans

Tip: A great idea for home is to create an organizational box—a place for extras such as posterboard, paper, glue, pencils, and markers.

Think of a place at home where you can study. It should be a place with good light and little noise or distractions. Also think of a place where you can put your homework and other school materials when you're finished studying—a spot where you can easily pick things up as you're dashing out the door to school. Then brainstorm ideas for solving these homework crises:

- With activities and homework, you have more than you can do in one night.
- You look in your backpack and find that you don't have the materials you need (examples: calculator, compass) to do your homework.

"Quiet, Please" Sign

pieces of tagboard (approx. 6" x 9") • markers • hole punch and yarn (optional)

Think of your study space at home. Is it a table in the kitchen? A desk in the living room? A corner of the bedroom? Take a sheet of tagboard. If you study in the kitchen or another family living area, fold the tagboard in half lengthwise so it can stand on a table or desk. If you study behind a closed door, punch a hole in the tagboard and tie a length of yarn to it. On your sign, write a study message such as "Quiet, Please," "Quiet, please, I'm studying," or "Thanks for being quiet while I study." Decorate the sign with your own special flair. Place your sign on your study table or desk, or hang it from your door.

Magic Message

copies of handout on page 92 • 6" x 6" sheets of paper • fine-line markers • colored pencils or markers

Make a "magic message" reminder to help you remember the guidelines and tools you need to get your homework done. Follow the directions on the handout. When you're finished, trade reminders with your classmates and compare notes on homework tools and strategies. Be sure to get your own back so you'll have it on hand when you need it.

Think About It, Talk About It

- Do you like having the support of someone who can review your homework or assist with your questions? Why or why not? Who could give you this support?

- What type of homework do you like best? Why?

- What type of homework is most difficult for you? Why? What might be some ways to make it easier?

Affirmation

I am learning the skills
to do homework successfully.

Resources

For Students

Romain, Trevor. *How to Do Homework Without Throwing Up* (Free Spirit Publishing, 1997). A humorous and useful book for kids. Ages 8–13.

Homework Checklist

Subject	Monday	Tuesday	Wednesday	Thursday	Friday
	Assignment Materials	Assignment Materials	Assignment Materials	Assignment Materials	Assignment Materials
	Assignment Materials	Assignment Materials	Assignment Materials	Assignment Materials	Assignment Materials
	Assignment Materials	Assignment Materials	Assignment Materials	Assignment Materials	Assignment Materials
	Assignment Materials	Assignment Materials	Assignment Materials	Assignment Materials	Assignment Materials

How to Make a "Magic Message" Homework Reminder

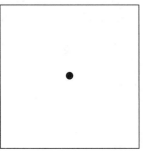

1

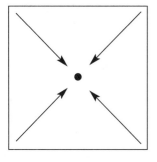

2

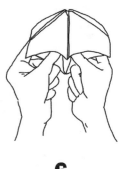

3

1. Put a dot in the exact center of a perfectly square piece of paper.
2. Take each corner and fold it into the center dot. Firmly crease each fold.
3. Turn the folded square over. Take each corner and fold it into the center of this side of the square.
4. Turn the square over again so the side with the center dot is facing you. Fold the square in half vertically (so the right side meets the left side).
5. Open the fold and fold the square in half horizontally (so the top meets the bottom).
6. Open the fold. Your square now has four "flaps." Put your thumbs and index fingers under the four flaps, gently lifting them. Pinch index finger to index finger, thumb to thumb.
7. Open your magic message reminder completely. Write messages and draw pictures in the different folded areas. Look at the example below, or come up with your own.
8. Repeat steps 2–7 to refold your magic message reminder.

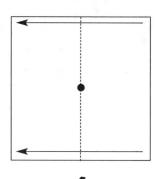

4

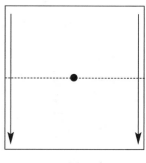

5

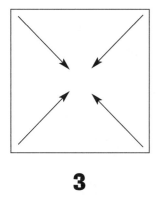

6

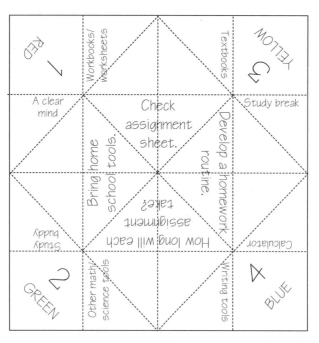

Getting Organized

"Organizing is what you do before you do something, so that when you do it, it's not all mixed up."

A.A. Milne (1882–1956), English author and playwright

If you've ever misplaced a shoe, a book, or an important assignment, you know what can happen when things aren't well organized. Do you shudder when you open your desk to look for a pencil? Give up rather than dig in your locker to find a book? A little practice in organization will help you stay on top of the details.

Note: Do the first two "Getting Organized" activities in sequence.

"Order" Talks

As a class, talk about how being organized can help people in school. Brainstorm ideas for keeping a desk, backpack, or locker organized. If you hear some tips that might work for you, jot them down.

Classroom Order

Take a few minutes to bring order to a part of your classroom. Ask your teacher what parts of the room need organizing. Then work in small groups to get the jobs done. Some possible places or items to put in order include bookshelves, art materials, play equipment, files, or storage areas.

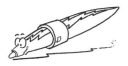

Inventories

An *inventory* is a list of all the things in one place. Make an inventory of the things you have in your desk, backpack, or locker. Write down all the items you have, and how many of each. Now take stock: Do you have everything you need? More than you need of certain items? What's missing? Is your desk, backpack, or locker well organized? Plan how you can better organize it to have all the things you need and find what you need easily. You may want to use ideas from the preceding activity.

Imaginary Hideaway

drawing paper • colored pencils or markers

Imagine a place of your own that could be your personal hideaway. It might be a tree house, a closet, a cave, or an underground den. What would you do in your fantasy hideaway? How would you organize your space? Draw a picture of yourself in your hideaway. Include in your drawing the things you would organize and keep there.

Scavenger Hunt

copies of handout on page 95

Tip: Before photocopying, customize the handout by adding additional items to be found in your classroom.

In small groups, work to locate the items on the list. Your goal is to determine where things are without letting other groups know where you've found them. For each item you find, write its location on the list. After ten minutes, compare lists with other groups. Was everyone able to find everything? How did the way the classroom is organized help you find the items you were looking for?

Think About It, Talk About It

- Do you think it's important to be organized? Why or why not?

- Is it possible to be too organized? Explain your answer.

- What past inventions have people come up with to help organize things? How have the inventions helped people?

- What might be some inventions that would help you be more organized?

- What is one area of your life that you would like to organize a little better? How are you going to do it?

Affirmation

I can get organized in ways that help me in school and at home.

For Students

Fox, Janet S. *Get Organized Without Losing It* (Free Spirit Publishing, 2005). Tips, lists, and strategies for staying on top of clutter and getting work done. Ages 8–13.

Schumm, Jeanne Shay. *School Power: Study Skill Strategies for Succeeding in School* (Free Spirit Publishing, 2001). This guide for school success covers everything kids need to know to develop strategies and organizational skills for coping with middle school or junior high. Ages 11 and up.

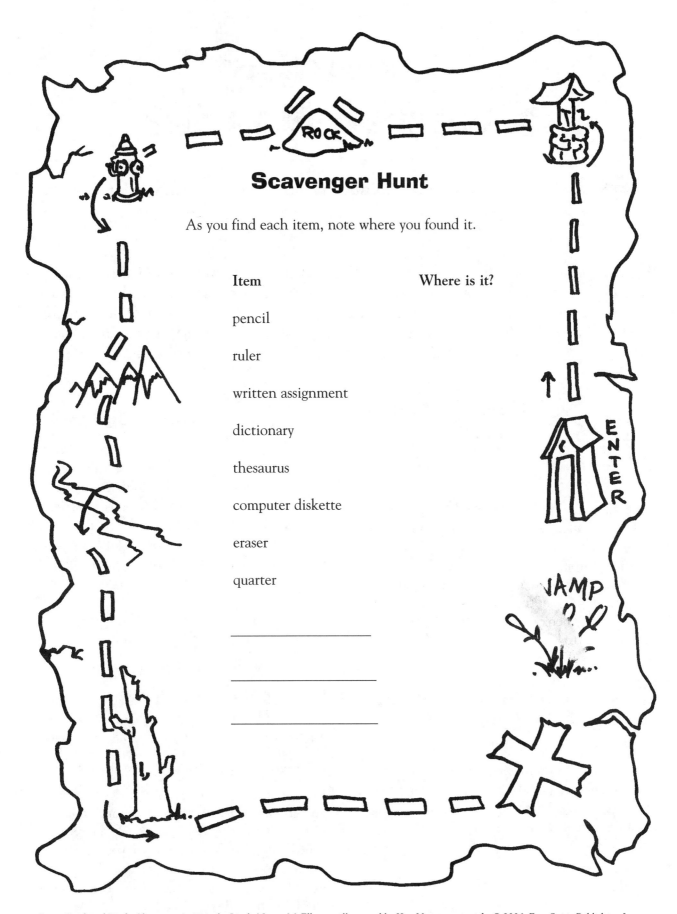

Scavenger Hunt

As you find each item, note where you found it.

Item	Where is it?
pencil	
ruler	
written assignment	
dictionary	
thesaurus	
computer diskette	
eraser	
quarter	
_____	
_____	
_____	

Becoming a Better Reader

"Those who don't read have no advantage over those who can't read."
Mark Twain (1835–1910), U.S. writer and humorist

Reading is a vital skill for school success. It's also a gateway to millions of stories and experiences that can spark your imagination, carry you to other parts of the world, satisfy your curiosity, and provide hours of adventure, humor, or simple fun. Whatever your interests might be, there are books that can tell you more about them. Through the reading that you do for enjoyment, you can enrich your reading skills for success in and out of school.

Book Treasure Chest

copies of handout on page 98 • colored pencils or markers

Finding a favorite book is like discovering treasure. Think about your favorite book. Why do you like it? Is it because of the characters? What did you learn from the book? How exciting is it to read? In the treasure chest on the handout, draw pictures of some of the things you like best about your favorite book—things that make it a "treasure" for you to keep and read again and again.

Favorite Book Talks

Volunteer to tell the class about your favorite book, why you like it, and why you would recommend it as a book others in the class will enjoy. See how well you can "sell" your favorite book.

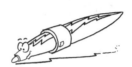

Book Genres

A *genre* is category or type of book, such as mystery, biography, fiction, or nonfiction. Do you have a favorite genre? When you go to the library, what kinds of books do you look for? Briefly talk about some of the genres you and others in your class enjoy. Then write a paragraph describing the kind of books you like to read best.

Decoding a Foreign Language

books or other reading materials in unfamiliar foreign language(s)

Tip: Besides checking your library or bookstore, you'll find foreign-language reading material in food packaging, appliance instructions, and museum pamphlets.

In small groups, try to read something written in a foreign language. After reading and talking it through for five minutes, have a volunteer from your group show the class what you've read and explain how you decided what it said. How did you figure out what the words mean? What are the clues that helped you "decode"?

Book Charades

3" x 5" file cards

Teacher: Prepare for this activity by writing titles of books your students will recognize on file cards. Write one book title per card. *Students:* Form groups of three or four. Draw a card and look at the book title you've selected. Keep it a secret from those who aren't in your group. Work with your group to pantomime the book title in a game of charades. Movements are fine, but no words are allowed.

Think About It, Talk About It

- Do you have a personal tip that helped improve your reading skill? Share it.

- What are some things you can do now that you couldn't do if you didn't know how to read?

- Do you think that parents, schools, and libraries should limit the kinds of books and magazines kids are allowed to read? Why or why not?

Affirmation

By learning what I like to read best,
I can become a better reader.

Resources

For Students

Miller, William, illustrations by Gregory Christie. *Richard Wright and the Library Card* (Lee & Low Books, 1999). Richard Wright lives in the segregated South in the 1920s. Because he is black, he cannot get a library card. A sympathetic co-worker assists, and Richard proceeds with his passion for reading, leading him to a career as a widely read and respected author. Based on a true story. Ages 6–9.

Spinelli, Jerry. *The Library Card* (Scholastic Press, 1997). Four unrelated tales demonstrate the power of reading and how the characters' lives were transformed once they used a library card to gain access to the world of books. Ages 11 and up.

For Teachers

American Library Association. The ALA provides a catalog of posters of illustrations from books and famous real-life characters that you can purchase. Contact your local library or write to ALA Graphics, American Library Association, 50 East Huron Street, Chicago, IL 60611. Toll-free phone: 1-800-545-2433, ext. 2426. Web site: www.alastore.ala.org

Book Treasure Chest

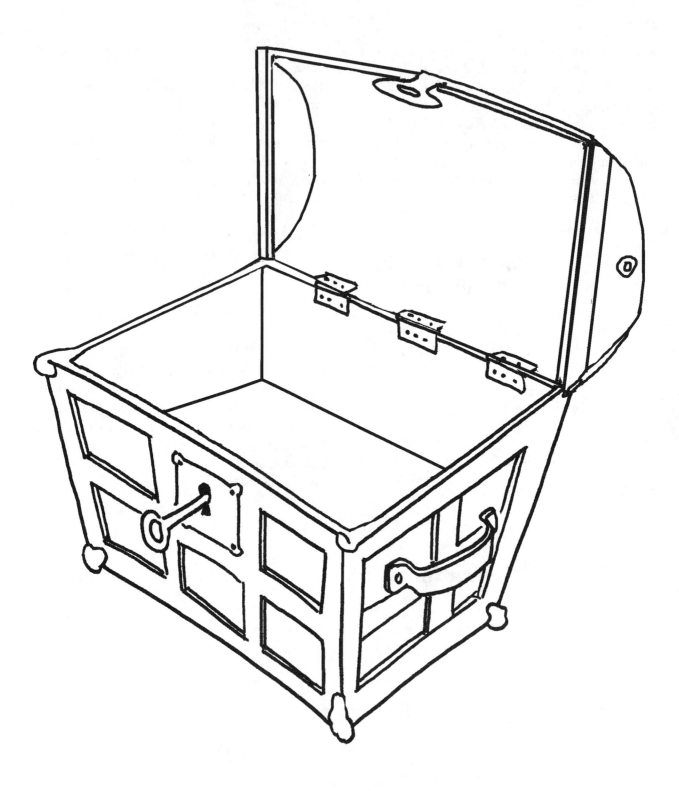

Thinking Creatively

"If you are seeking creative ideas, go out walking."
Raymond Inman, author

Every movement you make, every thought you think involves the creative powers of your mind. Whether you're working on a math problem, a science experiment, a book report, or a great new sports move, creativity comes into play. You can think of creativity as a kind of muscle that needs lots of exercise. The more you exercise it, the more creative you become. Let's give that muscle a workout!

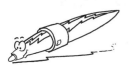

Silent Walk

With your teacher, take a silent, five-minute walk once around the school building, in front of the building, or through the halls. Don't speak. Instead, use your senses of sight, sound, and smell. When you return to your desk, write briefly about what you thought of while walking. How does walking in silence stimulate your thinking? If you wish, share what you've written with others in your class.

Script Treatments

When writers, directors, and producers plan a TV show, they start with a *script treatment*—an overall plan for what will happen in an episode. With everyone in the class, choose a TV show you're all familiar with. Then, in small groups, plan your own episode for the show, or come up with a different ending to a favorite episode. Describe or enact parts of your script treatments for the whole class. What different ideas came from the different groups?

Tangrams

copies of handout on page 101 • scissors • colored construction paper • glue

A *tangram* is a Chinese puzzle. It's made by cutting a square into five triangles, a square, and a *rhomboid*. Can you identify these shapes on the handout? (If you don't know what a rhomboid is, see if you can guess from looking at the handout. If you're still not sure, look it up in the dictionary.) Cut out the shapes and arrange them on a sheet of colored construction paper to create different figures, such as animals or birds. Once you find a shape you really like, glue it to the construction paper. Display the tangram figures and see how many different ways you and your classmates put the shapes together.

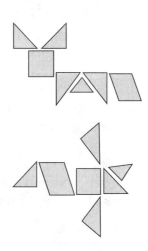

Marshmallow Structures

marshmallows • toothpicks

Do you remember the days when you built with blocks? Revisit your childhood with a new twist by building a structure using toothpicks and small marshmallows. Work in groups of two or three to craft unique buildings. Give your building a name. Discuss and compare the structures different groups have made. Arrange all the buildings together to create a marshmallow cityscape.

Creative Warm-Ups

Just like athletes, actors do warm-up exercises to get them into an acting mode. Get your body moving with some acting warm-ups. Use your own moves, or team up with others to become some of the following:

- a robot
- a bridge
- a tree
- the wind
- a train
- a spider
- a pair of scissors
- a skyscraper
- a butterfly
- an airplane
- a computer
- a boa constrictor

Think About It, Talk About It

- Do you think everyone is creative? Why or why not?

- Is creativity something that can be worked on and developed? Explain your answer.

- Do the games and toys of today encourage creative thinking? If you think they do, give examples and state how they help you think.

- What subjects in school do you think encourage your creative thinking? Why?

Affirmation

My creativity helps me see the world in different ways. I can use my brain power to be a creative thinker.

Resources

For Students

Armstrong, Thomas. *You're Smarter Than You Think* (Free Spirit Publishing, 2002). A kids' introduction to Howard Gardner's theory of multiple intelligences, this book focuses on how kids are smart, not how smart they are.

Madgwick, Wendy. *City Maze!* (Millbrook Press, 1995). View New York and eleven other international cities from the air. This book is packed with interesting information, unusual perspectives, and challenging mazes for readers to find their way through. Ages 8–11.

Tangram Shapes

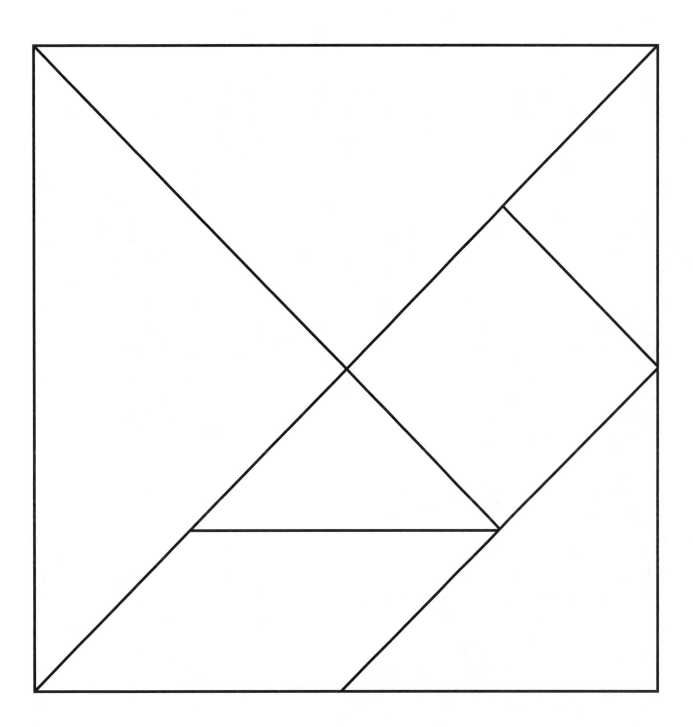

Surviving Tests

"If you think you can, you can."
Mary Kay Ash, U.S. businesswoman

Does the thought of a big test make your hands sweat and your heart race? If so, you're not alone. But tests don't need to be dreaded, anxiety-producing ordeals. Try some of the strategies in these activities to help you feel more relaxed and ready when test time rolls around.

Study Buddies

copies of handout on page 104

Team up with a partner. Look at the handout and talk together about how studying with a buddy could be helpful for each of you. If you have an upcoming test or quiz, study together for ten or fifteen minutes. One of you can be the coach, the other the learner. Then reverse roles. Use the end-of-chapter questions in your textbook or other study questions your teacher has provided.

Snack Bags

paper lunch bags • fine-line markers

When you're studying for a test, your body needs the right fuel to keep going. What energizing foods will help you do your best? On one side of a paper lunch bag, make a list of healthful study snacks that you enjoy. Try to include a mix of fruits and crackers or cereal, with a sprinkling of nuts or cheese. What can you drink as an energizing alternative to soda pop? On the other side, write a menu for your perfect night-before-the-test meal. Use your bag to carry snacks for studying at the library, in a corner or a room at home, or outdoors.

Following Directions

One of the first rules of test-taking is to read the directions carefully and completely and then follow them exactly. Here's a fun way to reinforce this rule. In small groups, write a simple set of "movement" directions. These should be something anyone could easily and safely do in your classroom. When you're done, trade directions with other groups. Read and follow each set of directions. Move and have fun!

1. Stand up.

2. Take two steps forward.

3. Spin clockwise 1-1/2 turns.

4. Walk four steps backward.

5. Walk six steps forward.

6. Sit back down in your seat.

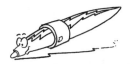

Test Do's and Don'ts

chart paper and marker

Break into small groups. Each group's challenge is to create a list of test-taking do's and don'ts. Half of the groups will write strategies for staying on top of studying day-to-day. (Example: *"Don't* wait to study till the last minute. *Do* study a bit each day.") The other half will write tips for actually taking the test. (Example: *"Don't* panic when you don't know an answer. *Do* move on to the next question.") Post the guidelines for all to see, or photocopy them so you can each have your own copy.

Drawing a Good Night's Sleep

copies of handout on page 105 • colored pencils or fine-line markers

On the night before a test, you need a good night's sleep. On the handout, fill in the three-frame cartoon strip. Put words or pictures in the thought bubbles for each frame. How can taking the time to prepare and imagining yourself doing well help you succeed? If you're a natural worrier, keep these thoughts in mind: Tests make up only part of your grade. Do your best with other efforts, too, such as discussions, written assignments, and projects. Believe in yourself.

Think About It, Talk About It

• Besides giving tests, what other ways could a teacher test your knowledge and know-how?

• Do you feel worried before a test? What are some things you can do to feel more relaxed and prepared?

• After you've completed a tough test, have you ever vowed to do something different next time? If so, what?

Affirmation

I can handle tests by preparing and following through on a plan.

Resources

For Students

Kesselman-Turkel, Judi, and Franklynn Peterson. *Test-Taking Strategies* (University of Wisconsin Press, 2004). Provides strategies for multiple-choice, true-false, oral, and essay tests and offers ways to handle anxiety and manage time. Ages 11 and up.

For Teachers

Schumm, Jeanne Shay. *How to Help Your Child with Homework* (Free Spirit Publishing, 2005). A thorough book to read yourself and share with parents. It includes guidelines for handling tests as well as strategies for specific subject areas such as math, reading, spelling, writing, science, social studies, and foreign languages.

Study Buddy Guidelines for Test Preparation

1. Select a classmate you work well with and who has the same study goals.

2. Plan short, frequent study sessions rather than one long one.

3. Choose a quiet location with few distractions, such as a bedroom at home or the library.

4. Agree ahead of time about what material you'll cover.

5. Decide how much time to spend on each subject. Then stick to your time allotment.

6. Take turns asking and answering questions.

Drawing a Good Night's Sleep

Show yourself sleeping the night before the test. You're relaxed, not restless.

Show yourself taking the test. You're calm, not tense.

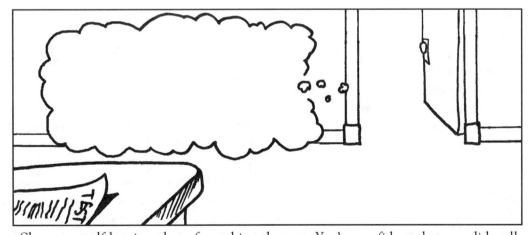

Show yourself leaving class after taking the test. You're confident that you did well.

What I Want My Teacher to Know

"How we learn is what we learn."
Bonnie Friedman, U.S. author, in *Writing Past Dark*

Teachers know many ways to make school an exciting place for learning—and so do kids. Here's your chance to tell your teacher some of your ideas for making school a great place to be.

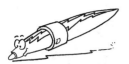

A Suggestion for the Teacher

Are there ways you think your teacher could make school a better place? Think about it. Then write a paragraph that completes this sentence: "If I could tell my teacher one thing that would make school better for me and others, this is what I'd say."

A Letter to Your Teacher

small mailing envelopes

Just like you, teachers enjoy getting positive feedback. What do you appreciate most about your teacher? Take a moment to write a letter telling her or him about it. To keep your letter private, put it in an envelope when you're done, seal it, and place it in the mailbox (see next activity) or an "in basket" on the teacher's desk.

Mailbox Stamps

drawing paper cut to approx. 2" x 3" • colored pencils or markers • glue • box (any size)

Tip: Cut the paper with pinking shears for a stamp-like edge.

Help decorate a mailbox that can hold notes and suggestions from you and others to your teacher. On a 2" x 3" piece of drawing paper, draw your own unique stamp design. Glue it to the box your teacher has supplied. Use the box for "mailing" notes to your teacher—requests for help, thank yous, or suggestions.

Trading Places

Do you have a sure way to present a lesson to your classmates? Volunteer to teach a short lesson to a group of students. You might describe how to solve a math problem, explain a grammar rule, or lead a discussion about a social studies topic. As you present your lesson, your teacher will move from group to group, observing the teaching styles of you and others. You'll learn what it takes to be a teacher—and your teacher will probably learn something from you.

Joke Time

Let your teacher in on some of your favorite jokes. Two simple rules apply: The jokes should have a "G" rating, and they shouldn't intentionally hurt anyone's feelings. Take turns telling favorite jokes, riddles, limericks, and stories. Invite your teacher to take a turn, too. Laughter's good for everyone!

Think About It, Talk About It

- Imagine that you're an adult. You're standing in front of your own class or children. What do you want them to learn in school? Why?

- Do you think teachers appreciate comments from the class? Why or why not?

- What are some other ways to let your teacher know what you're thinking?

Affirmation

I will let my teacher in on my thoughts about school and about myself.

Resources

For Students

Dahl, Michael, illustrations by Garry Nichols. *School Daze: A Book of Riddles About School* (Picture Window Books, 2003). Jokes and more jokes. Why did the student bring a ladder to music class? The teacher told him to sing higher. Ages 4–9.

Lansky, Bruce, illustrations by Stephen Carpenter. *No More Homework! No More Tests! Kids' Favorite Funny School Poems* (Meadowbrook Press, 1997). Humorous poetry that gets to the bottom of kids' feelings about school. Ages 8–12.

Weintraub, Aileen. *The Everything Kids' Knock Knock Book* (Adams Media, 2004). Knock knock jokes are silly, simple, and sure to please.

For Teachers

Bluestein, Jane, comp. *Mentors, Masters, and Mrs. MacGregor* (Health Communications, 1995). A delightful collection of stories, by people of all ages and from all walks of life, applauding the efforts of teachers and the difference these teachers have made in their lives.

What's Right with School?

"I think that education is power."

Oprah Winfrey, U.S. talk show host and actress

School is just the right place to meet and make friends, a place where you can take chances and try new things. Somewhere in your school there's a teacher, a subject, a class, or an activity that you look forward to and enjoy. Here's your chance to speak up and take pride in the best parts of your school.

School Trees

drawing paper • colored pencils or markers

A family tree records your biological history. Create your own "school tree" as a way to record the good experiences and memories from your years in school. On a large sheet of drawing paper, draw a simple tree. Start with the trunk, and then draw branches for every year you've spent in school. Label each branch with a grade, a teacher's name, or a few words that tell something great about that particular school year. Color or decorate the tree branches to show friends, fun activities, and exciting learning that took place for you.

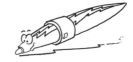

School Plaques

copies of handout on page 110 • colored pencils or markers

History has its legends: George Washington, Harriet Tubman, Elizabeth Cady Stanton. Your school has its special people, too. Honor someone in your school by creating a plaque suitable for gracing the walls of the hall or classroom. Who in your school deserves a plaque? Yourself? A principal? A teacher? A custodian? Write a fitting tribute on the handout. If you wish, add decorative art. Display the plaque so the honored person can see it.

School Cheers

Does your school have an official school cheer? Here's your chance to cheer it, change it, or make one up. In small groups, think of short, simple cheers that say something great about your school. Perform the cheers for the rest of the class. Enjoy sharing your school spirit!

Items That Will Make History

Have you ever been to a museum that showed items from school days of the past? Inkwells, slates, and copybooks have all taken their place in history. Look around your classroom. What things do you think will be in a museum fifty years from now? Take turns presenting your thoughts on some of your classroom's future museum pieces.

Word Collage

large sheets of posterboard • colorful markers, ink pens, or fine-line markers

What are the words that describe what's right about school? Think of three things. Take a few minutes to plan a way to write about them art-fully—with calligraphy, block letters, or another imaginative method. Using brightly colored markers, write your three words or phrases on a class poster. Be artistic! See if you can get permission to post the word collage in the school entrance, where others can admire your work and consider what's right with school.

Think About It, Talk About It

- What are the best classes or subjects in your school? Why?

- What makes a school a pleasant place to be?

- What makes a classroom a comfortable place where you can enjoy learning?

- What makes a good teacher?

- How do the people in the classroom help make it a good or bad place to be?

Affirmation

There's a lot that's good about my school. I can enjoy and build on those things.

Resources

For Students

Dahl, Roald. *Matilda* (Puffin Books, 1998). Matilda, who loves school, finds a mentor in her creative and understanding teacher. This book is filled with schoolroom humor and slapstick. Ages 9–12.

For Teachers

Glasser, William. *The Quality School Teacher* (HarperPerennial, 1998). The author promotes creating a cooperative and friendly classroom environment with a focus on useful work.

Mitchell, Craig, and Pamela Espeland. *Teach to Reach: Over 300 Strategies, Tips, and Helpful Hints for Teachers of All Grades* (Free Spirit Publishing, 1996). Insights and ideas presented in this book will make school more meaningful and enjoyable for everyone.

School Plaque

What's Wrong with School?

"No more pencils! No more books! No more teachers' dirty looks!"
Anonymous

It's one thing to complain about school. It's another thing to identify a problem and think about ways to change it. Here's your chance to do both—with humor and some serious thinking.

Note: Do the last three "What's Wrong with School?" activities in sequence.

A New School Schedule

How would you change your school schedule to make each day better for you? Would you have twice the computer time and half the math time? Would you eat lunch a little later? Write your own personal plan for a school day that's right from start to finish.

Problem-Solving Skits

In groups, develop short skits in which the characters make something that's wrong with school right. Here are some ideas for themes: a crowded lunchroom, a crabby substitute teacher, too much homework, no gum-chewing rule, or long assemblies. Volunteer to act out your skit for the class. Do you think any of the groups' ideas would help make school a better place?

One Thing I Don't Like

drawing paper • colored pencils or markers • tape

Do you always like being in school? When you don't, why don't you want to be there? Think about one thing that feels wrong with school from your point of view. Draw a circle in the middle of a sheet of paper. Inside the circle, draw a picture that shows this thing you don't like about school. Tape your sheet with others along the top or bottom edge of the board. You'll use them in two more activities.

Ideas for Fixing What's Wrong

drawings from the preceding activity • chart paper and marker

Look at what you and your classmates drew about what's wrong with school. Have some people noted the same problems? Choose a problem and talk about ways to make what's wrong *right*. List your ideas on chart paper. If you think you've come up with enough good ideas to solve a problem, draw a line through the circles that talked about that wrong thing. Keep the problems posted and continue to look for ways to make what's wrong with school right.

Taking Action

Think about the problems you've talked about and some of the suggestions for changing what's wrong with school. Choose one problem you care about and feel you have a good idea for solving. Write a proposal to your teacher, principal, or school board outlining the problem and suggesting a way to make it right. Ask your teacher for the best way to deliver your proposal.

Think About It, Talk About It

- Did everyone agree about what's wrong with school and what would help make it right? If not, why?

- Was there a particular issue raised by many people that you would like to address some more? What are some ways you can work with students or adults in the school to help fix the problem?

- Do you think it's possible to make school feel right for everyone all the time? Why or why not?

- Why do you think different schools have different schedules, rules, and ways of doing things?

Affirmation

I can take positive steps to make my school a better place for me.

Resources

For Students

Toles, Tom. *My School Is Worse Than Yours* (Viking, 1999). There's no school worse than Raven's, with a rusty robot for a teacher and a building that's completely underground. Ages 8–12.

Learning New Words

"If the English language made any sense, lackadaisical would have something to do with a shortage of flowers."

Doug Larson, U.S. writer

While we communicate in many different ways, words are one of the most powerful. The greater your vocabulary, the more ways you have to say what you mean and be understood. To develop this strength, team up with classmates. Have some fun while you stretch your vocabulary.

Notes: *Teacher:* Before doing these activities, you'll want to compile a list of unfamiliar vocabulary words. Use as many words as you have students in the class. Write each word in pen on the front of a 3" x 5" envelope. Stock the classroom with dictionaries, thesauruses, and vocabulary-building software and books.

Do the "Learning New Words" activities in sequence.

Partner Words

the word envelopes • slips of paper (approx. 8" x 2")

Team up with a partner. Choose two envelopes. You'll find a word—probably an unfamiliar one—written across the front of each. Consider one word at a time. Do you know what it means? Can you guess? If not, look up the word in the dictionary. On a slip of paper, write the meaning of the word and place the slip in the envelope. Together, write a sentence on the back of the envelope that uses the new word. Repeat the process to figure out the second word. Save the envelopes for four more activities.

Group Words

the word envelopes

Share your words and sentences (but not the definitions!) from the first activity with the rest of the class. Can others guess each word's meaning from *context*—the way it's used in the sentence? Open the envelope and read the definition. Did some people guess correctly? Continue with the other words from the first activity. Put the definitions back in the envelopes and save them for three more activities.

Beat the Clock

the word envelopes

Alone or with a partner, select a word envelope. Review the word's definition and plan how you will act out the meaning. You can use pantomime, sound effects, speech, riddles, synonyms (words that have the same meaning), or any other approach that suits your word. Allow no more than one minute for acting out and guessing each word. When you're done, replace the definitions in the envelopes. Save the envelopes for two more activities.

Rebus Puzzles

the word envelopes

A *rebus* uses pictures or symbols to represent a word. With a partner, choose a word envelope. Together, create a rebus puzzle about the word. You might use the word only, or a short sentence that includes it. Have fun with this. When you're through, display the rebus puzzles so others can figure them out. Save the envelopes for one more activity.

houseboat

The houseboat sailed
down the Mississippi River.

Word Game

the word envelopes

Choose one of the envelopes, keeping it secret. The last person to draw a word begins the game by saying, "My teacher publishes a dictionary, and in it is a _____-letter word that begins with the letter ___. It means _____."
Others guess. The first person to correctly identify the word takes the next turn, giving clues about his or her word. Continue until every word has been used or time is up.

Think About It,
Talk About It

- Do you enjoy expanding your vocabulary? Why or why not?

- What makes you interested in a word?

- What helps you learn and remember new words?

- Have you recently added a word to your vocabulary? Share it with the group. Explain the word's meaning and tell where you heard or saw it first.

- Noah Webster published his first dictionary in the 1800s. Since then, the dictionary has been updated many times. Why do you think dictionaries need updating? What are some words that are probably new to the time you live in? Can you spell them and define them?

Affirmation

Learning and using new words gives me
more ways to express myself.

Resources

For Students

Clements, Andrew, illustrations by Brian
Selznick. *Frindle* (Simon & Schuster, 1998). A
humorous story about a boy who changes the
word for pencil, to the great dismay of his teacher
and school. Ages 8–12.

Sherk, William. *500 Years of New Words* (Doubleday & Co., 2004). A fascinating book of facts
on how, when, and why popular words first
appeared in the English language. Examples: *zit*
(1975), *workaholic* (1971), *ski* (1885), *dinosaur*
(1841), *pajamas* (1800), *denim* (1695), and *pet*
(1508). All ages.

For Teachers

Thurston, Cheryl Miller. *Surviving Last Period on
Fridays and Other Desperate Situations: Cottonwood
Game Book for Language Arts* (Cottonwood Press,
2003). An excellent collection of language arts
activities including exercises using the dictionary
and many lessons designed to encourage interest
in words and word usage. For middle school.

What I Want
to Learn About

"What we learn with pleasure we never forget."
Charles Alfred Mercier (1816–1894), U.S. doctor and writer

Learning isn't something you only do in school or when you're young—it's a lifetime activity. Your teachers may follow lesson plans, but you can do some planned learning on your own, as well. What are you curious about? What would you like to become an expert in? Let's find out!

Note: Do the "What I Want to Learn About" activities in sequence.

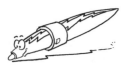

Learning "Notices"

writing paper cut to exactly 4" x 5" • colored pencils or markers (optional)

Have you seen notices nailed to telephone poles or taped in store windows? People post notices when they've lost a pet, have something for sale, or want to let others know about an event. On a 4" x 5" sheet of paper, write your own notice regarding one thing that you are curious about or want to learn about. Your notice can be simply written or highly decorated—it's up to you. Save your notice for the next activity.

Accordion Book

copies of handout on page 118 • sheets of 8½" x 11" paper • scissors • 4" x 5" pieces of cardboard • 12" lengths of ribbon or string, 2 for each student • tape • glue • notices from preceding activity

To learn more about something, it helps to have a plan. Make a simple accordion book that you can use for writing notes and collecting information. Follow the directions on the handout. Glue your notice on the cover. On the first page, write "Suggestions from kids in my class." Save your book for the next activity.

Information Wanted

Wish to learn all I can about the Loch Ness Monster

Sharing Information

the accordion books

Share your accordion book with others in the class. Pass it around and ask others to write ideas that could help you learn about your topic (examples: book titles, magazine articles, names of stores or store addresses, personal advice). While your book is being passed along, look at each book that comes your way. If you see one or two subjects you know something about, jot suggestions inside those books. Sign your name after your suggestions. Return the books to their owners and save them for two more activities.

Learning More

the accordion books

Look at the ideas people wrote in your accordion book. Move around the room, talking to people whose ideas were helpful and asking for more information. Carry your pencil with you and jot down notes in your book. Save the book for one more activity.

Making a Plan

the accordion books

Review the ideas on your own. Make a plan for how you'll pursue your interest. You might number the suggestions you got, starting with what seems easiest or most important to do. On a blank page in your book, write a plan or a simple outline of how you'll go about learning about your interest. Keep the accordion book and use it to make notes and store information as you learn more about your subject.

Think About It, Talk About It

- Do you think people stop learning when they finish school? Explain your answer.

- Is there anyone you know who has a desire to learn something? How could you help?

- Look up the word *mentor* in the dictionary. Do you know of a mentor who could help you or someone else in the group with what you want to learn about? Be specific.

Affirmation

I can take charge of learning about something that really interests me.

Resources

For Students

Erlbach, Arlene. *The Kids' Invention Book* (Lerner Publications, 1999). True stories about successful inventions by kids.

World Almanac for Kids. This site has fun facts, games, and explorations for everything from inventions to animals. Ages 8 and up. Web site: www.worldalmanacforkids.com

How to Make an Accordion Book

1. Fold a sheet of 8½" x 11" paper in half lengthwise. Cut along the fold.

2. Fold each small sheet of paper 3 times into 4 accordion folds.

3. Use two 4" x 5" pieces of cardboard for the cover. Securely tape or glue ribbons onto one side of each cardboard cover.

4. Glue your notice to one of the cover pieces, on the side where there is no ribbon. This will be the outside cover of your accordion file.

5. Unfold the two sheets of paper. Tape the two sheets together at the short side, as shown. You should now have eight folds of paper.

6. Securely glue the first and last fold of paper to the covers, as shown.

7. Let the glue dry. Later, fold the book and tie both sides to close it.

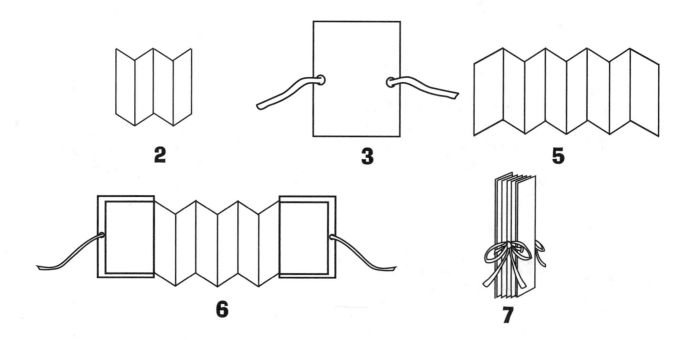

Setting Goals

"Goals are dreams with deadlines."
Diana Scharf Hunt, U.S. motivational writer

Do you have big dreams for yourself? To reach them, you need to set goals. Short-term goals can help you accomplish the things you want to do today or this week. Often these short-term goals will take you, a step at a time, toward achieving what you want over a month, a year, or a lifetime. Get ready to set a course for reaching both small goals and large ones.

Cinquain Poem

copies of handout on page 122

A *cinquain* is a five-line poem that doesn't rhyme. Each line has a set number of syllables. Alone or in small groups, think of a goal you want to set (examples: not putting off studying, getting up in time to eat a good breakfast). Using the handout as a guide, write a cinquain poem about that goal.

A Goal You've Been Putting Off

What is one thing you've been meaning to do, but just haven't gotten around to? Do you want to clean a messy bedroom? Write a letter to a faraway friend? Finish building a model? Set the goal for yourself. Write yourself a promise telling what your goal is, how you're going to accomplish it, and the date when you'll have it done. Tape your promise in a place where it will remind you of your goal. Follow through and enjoy the satisfaction of setting and meeting a personal goal.

A Goal Close to Home

Do you have a grandparent who'd love to hear from you? A neighbor who'd enjoy a little company? A sister or brother who keeps asking you to play a game? In small groups, talk about some of these people. Share ideas for ways to spend enjoyable time with someone special. Then plan what you'll do with this person. Make it a goal to act on your plan by a certain time, such as before the weekend or within the next week. Follow through and see how satisfying it can be to reach out to someone close to you.

Totem Poles

squares of strong cardboard (approx. 3" x 3") • empty paper-towel tubes • glue • drawing paper • colored pencils or markers • scissors

Native people of North America used totem poles to tell the stories of their lives and accomplishments. Borrow from this tradition and create your own totem pole that tells the story of one of your life goals. First, glue a square cardboard base to an empty paper-towel tube. Next, draw small pictures that represent your goal. (Example: If you want to play on the varsity football squad someday, you might draw a football, school letter, and helmet, write some of the words to your local high school's song, and add some scraps of your school colors.) Cut them out and glue them to the tube, beginning at the bottom. Let your totem pole decorate a desk or dresser at home, where it can remind you of the goal you want to reach.

Balance Challenge

hardcover books

Do you set goals when you exercise? Here's a balancing exercise that will show you how to set small goals in order to improve a bit at a time. Standing next to your desk, close your eyes and raise one foot. How long can you hold it? Repeat, this time raising the other foot. Now stand on both feet, place a book on top of your head, and close your eyes. How long can you keep the book in place? Choose the balance challenge that's most difficult for you, and keep practicing, each time trying to balance a little longer than before. For example, if standing on your left foot with your eyes closed is difficult, start by standing on both feet. Slowly lift your right foot and count to two. Repeat, this time counting to three. Continue, working to extend the time you can keep your balance. What does this exercise tell you about ways to accomplish difficult goals?

Think About It, Talk About It

- Do you think it's important to have goals? Why or why not?

- Is it possible to set a goal for yourself that is too difficult? Explain your answer.

- Have you ever set a goal for yourself and reached it? Tell how you achieved your goal.

- Think of someone you admire, such as a parent, a celebrity, an athlete, or a friend. What goal do you think that person set and worked toward?

Affirmation

I'll set a goal that I can work toward. I can set smaller goals to help me along the way.

Resources

For Students

Rockwell, Thomas. *How to Eat Fried Worms* (Cornerstone Books, 2003). In this classic humorous tale, Billy is willing to set his sights high to win fifty dollars for a minibike. Ages 9–12.

For Teachers

Jensen, Vickie. *Carving a Totem Pole* (Henry Holt & Co., 1996). This account describes the various steps in carving and raising a totem pole as done by Nisga'a artist Norman Tait. You may want to read this account to students.

Cinquain
Poem

Here's an example of a cinquain poem:

Breakfast.
I will get up
Each day at seven sharp
To eat a great breakfast that makes
Me full.

Here's the same poem, syllable by syllable:

Break - fast. (2)
I will get up (4)
Each day at se - ven sharp (6)
To eat a great break - fast that makes (8)
Me full. (2)

Write your own cinquain poem.
Use each line for one syllable:

_____ _____

_____ _____ _____ _____

_____ _____ _____ _____ _____ _____

_____ _____ _____ _____ _____ _____ _____ _____

_____ _____

Getting Support

"My mother was the one who made me work, made me believe that one day it would be possible for me to walk without braces."

—Wilma Rudolph, U.S. Olympic gold medalist in track and field

Getting through the "growing up" years requires support from special people. We all need to know that there's someone to lean on for help and guidance or just to be there by our side. Who are your supporters? What are some creative ways to ask for help and encouragement and to say thank you for that support? Let's find out!

Note: Do the second and third "Getting Support" activities in sequence.

Helper Art

drawing paper • colored pencils or markers

Help and understanding when you need it most might come from a parent, a relative, or a friend. Draw a picture of yourself and the supportive person you have, or want to have, to depend on. While you draw, talk about the ways you and others in your class discovered (and can discover) this kind of support.

Help Request

writing paper cut to 4" x 5"

Are you feeling the need for a little support right now? Do you have a tough assignment in school, a problem with a friend, or a worry that keeps nagging? Think of someone you know and trust who might be able to offer support and guidance. Write a short note to that person on a 4" x 5" sheet of paper. State what support you need and how it will help you. Save the message for the next activity.

Dear Big Brother,
I need some help reviewing social studies. It'll help me pass the test next week. Could you help?
Thanks.
Nima

Paper Homing Pigeons

copies of handout on page 125 • notes from preceding activity • stapler • heavy paper, such as tagboard or posterboard • colored pencils or markers • scissors • hole punch • yarn or string • paper clips

For centuries, homing pigeons have carried messages from town to town, asking for assistance. Create your own paper homing pigeon to deliver the message you wrote asking for support. Follow the directions on the handout. When you deliver the messenger bird, tell the person you're sending an important message via homing pigeon. Find a place to keep and hang the bird, and use it in the future for delivering other messages.

Clapping

Clapping is a way of giving support. The ancient Egyptians used clapping to entertain people working in the fields or fishing. Today we clap for athletes, dancers, and other performers, telling them that we like what they're doing and appreciate the effort they're making. Get some applause from your classmates by describing something you're proud of. It might be an assignment you worked hard on, the way you helped someone, or a goal you set and met. Volunteer to speak, and encourage others to volunteer as well. After each person talks, clap hard and long to show your support.

Help for Different Things

You get different kinds of support from different people. Who helps you when you're struggling with music lessons? With sports plays? With a tricky math assignment? Whom do you turn to when you're having problems with friends? When you're worried or scared? Think of three people in your life who give you support at different times. If you like, tell the group about these people and the specific things they do to support you in your day-to-day life. Plan to write a note or give a call to let these people know you appreciate what they do for you.

Dad,
Trying out for the play wasn't so bad after all. Thanks for going over the script with me.
Love,
Carrie

Think About It, Talk About It

- Do you think it's possible to get along without support from other people? Explain your answer.

- Who are some adults you can turn to when you're struggling with a big problem?

- What are some ways to let others know that you want or need their support?

- What are some ways you can support others?

- Besides through adults, friends, and family, where else can you find support?

Affirmation

I can ask for and find support when I need it.

Resources

For Teachers

Boys and Girls Clubs of America. Over 2,000 clubs nationwide offer encouragement and support for young people. Check your local white pages in the telephone book, or call the national headquarters for assistance at 1-800-854-CLUB (1-800-854-2582). Web site: www.bgca.org

How to Make a Homing Pigeon

1. Fold your note back and forth, like a fan. The folds should be thin and of the same width.

2. Staple the middle of the folded paper. Set it aside—it will become the wings of the bird.

3. Draw a bird's body on heavy paper. Use the sample here as a pattern. Cut it out.

4. Cut a slit at the bottom of the bird's body and punch a hole above the slit.

5. Slip the fanned note into the slit and spread the folds outward to form wings.

6. Loop a piece of yarn or string through the hole.

7. Bend a paper clip into an "S" form and attach it to the top of the yarn.

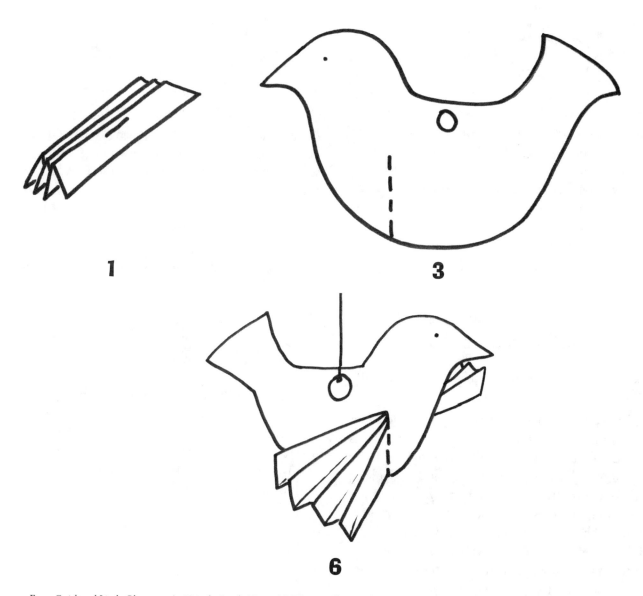

1

3

6

Imagining My Future

"I'm a 'will-be.'"
Lauren Bacall, U.S. actress

The future is full of possibilities. Now is a perfect time for you to "try on" different careers and find out how they might fit the future you.

Note: Do the second and third "Imagining My Future" activities in sequence.

Journalistic Questions

Think for a minute about the kinds of things you hope to do in the future—about a future job, activities you plan to enjoy for fun, or places you hope to go. If you could talk to a person who is living your future dream right now, what would you want to know? Develop a list of questions you would ask, using these journalistic questions: Who? What? Where? When? Why? How? Follow through by asking someone who might have the answers.

Career Art

drawing paper • colored pencils or markers • cards from preceding activity • tape or glue

Draw yourself in your future career. What will you be wearing? Where will you be working? Are you wearing a space suit on a space station? A judge's robe in a courtroom? A uniform on a naval ship? A leotard on a trapeze? Leave room to tape or glue your file card in the bottom left-hand corner of your drawing. Display the labeled drawings. How have your classmates imagined their future careers?

Searching the Want Ads

want-ad sections from several Sunday newspapers • 3" x 5" file cards • scissors • stapler

In the "Classifieds" section of the newspaper you'll find *want ads*. Search the Sunday want ads to see if there's a job that sounds right for the future you. First, write your name and a couple of interests on a file card. Alone or with a partner, read the ads, looking for jobs that interest you. (Hint: The ads are alphabetized.) Can you find a job you wouldn't mind trying? Something that interests you now and may in the future? Cut out the ad or make a copy. Staple it to your card. Save the card for one more activity.

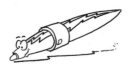

Tongue Twisters

Imagine yourself twenty years in the future. Write a *tongue twister* about something you see yourself doing. Tongue twisters repeat letters or sounds in a way that can be hard to pronounce. Nonsense words are fine, too. Share your tongue twisters with others, and try some of theirs as well.

A doodling dentist does drawings of dentures and dimples.

Perfect parent practices patience in permitting pillow fights.

Future Play Acting

Think of something you want to do as a career or for fun sometime in the distant future. Think of someone, famous or not, who has that career or does that activity. Imitate that person, using words, gestures, and movements. Have others ask questions as they try to guess who or what you are. Be as serious or silly as you like.

Think About It, Talk About It

- When you think about your future, where do you get your ideas? From adults you know and like? From books, TV, movies, the Internet, or music? From friends? How do these different people and things give you ideas for the future? Be specific.

- Do you think it's important to think about your future? Why or why not?

- Do you think it's important to have a career that you like? Explain your answer.

- Think of the one person in the world whom you would like to model your life after. Who is it? What qualities does this person have that you'd like to develop? Why?

Affirmation

I can dream and learn today about the future I want to have tomorrow.

Resources

For Students

Careers for Kids Cards (Table Talk, 1997). Four card decks (art, music, sports, and technology) introduce more than 160 professions. Each card tells an interesting fact or story about the career, offers an open-ended question for conversation, and provides an action idea kids can follow to learn more about the career. All ages.

Duggleby, John. *Artist in Overalls: The Life of Grant Wood* (Chronicle Books, 1995). This book for young people retraces the artist's life from early childhood. Learn what interests led Grant Wood down the path to develop an American style of painting, called *regionalism*. Wood's famous painting, "American Gothic," provides a perfect model for the "Career Art" activity. Ages 9–13.

Terban, Marvin, illustrations by Giulio Maestro. *It Figures! Fun Figures of Speech* (Clarion Books, 1993). Figures of speech such as alliteration (tongue twisters) are introduced by way of great writers, along with suggestions on how to imagine your own words. Ages 9–12.

Many Ways to Communicate

"The two words 'information' and 'communication' are often used interchangeably, but they signify quite different things. Information is giving out; communication is getting through."

Sydney J. Harris, U.S. writer and columnist

There are many ways to communicate. Spoken words, body gestures, and facial expressions all define your thoughts and feelings. Yet often when people communicate, they don't see and hear the same things. Get ready to learn and practice ways to say what you mean and to have your communication welcomed and understood.

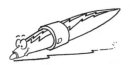 ## I-Statements

Mother Teresa, a nun and missionary who devoted her life to helping the sick and the outcast, once said, "Kind words can be short and easy to speak, but their echoes are truly endless." Sometimes, though, kind words aren't the ones that first occur to us. When friends disagree, it can be easy to say unkind or overly critical things, like "You're so mean!" or "You make me mad!" Rather than help solve a problem, hurtful words usually make both people more upset. What can you say instead? "I-statements" let you tell what's bothering you, how you feel about it, and why you feel that way—all without blaming. Read the examples below. What makes them feel more friendly? Working with a partner, come up with I-statements you can use when talking about problems. When you're done, compare the different I-statements. Did you find lots of ways to get your points across? Examples:

- "When you look in my backpack without asking, I get upset, because it's private."
- "I don't like it when someone takes food from my tray. I wish you'd ask me if you want something."

 ## Body Language

A particular way you sit or slouch, how you move around, your smile or pout—all of these movements communicate something about you. Play with face and body gestures to communicate without words. Try showing a few of these:

- "Sure."
- "We won!"
- "You're cute!"
- "So long."
- "I'm amazed."
- "I'm terrified!"

- "No way."
- "I come in peace."
- "Hi there."
- "Great job!"
- "That's not so good."
- "I'm sorry."

 ## Listening

Did you know that listening is hard for many people? Here's an exercise that can help you build listening skills. Form groups of three. You'll each get a turn being the speaker, the listener, and the watcher. Speakers talk to the listeners for one or two minutes. They talk about something of interest to them (examples: a great movie they saw, how they're going to spend their weekend, or why they're interested in collecting bugs). Listeners use these good listening skills:

- Sit quietly.
- Look at the speaker.
- Ask questions.
- Repeat things to make sure you understand.

Watchers notice how the listeners listen, using the four skills as a guide. When each person has had a chance to do all three tasks, talk with the whole class about what you've learned about being a good listener.

Handwriting Analysis

copies of handout on page 130 • some recent written work

The words that you select for a school assignment show your understanding of the lesson. But the way you write those words may say even more! Pull out some written work you've done recently. Examine the size, shape, and slant of your letters and words. Use the handout to learn what the way you write says about your personality. Examine your own handwriting or someone else's.

Universal Pictures

drawing paper • colored pencils or markers

Some pictures are used all over the country or around the world to give messages everyone understands. Talk briefly about some of these universal symbols (examples: signs that mean "No smoking," "Restrooms," "Poison," or "Please clean up after your dog"). Come up with a simple symbol to represent something. Use your ideas to represent "Lunchroom," "Bedtime," "Keep Out," and other ideas you think of. When you're done, look at your classmates' symbols. Does everyone understand each one? Share ideas for making the symbols easy for all to understand.

Think About It, Talk About It

- When you have strong feelings, is it better to just say what you're feeling or to think before you speak? Explain your answer.

- Do you think that someday the world will communicate using one language? If not, how will people understand each other? If so, will that be a good thing? Why or why not?

- In parts of India it's considered rude to point your feet at another person. In some cultures, people bow to show respect. What other face and body gestures do you know about that are different from the way you do things in your own part of the world?

Affirmation

In everything I do, I communicate. I can take care to communicate clearly and respectfully.

Resources

For Students

Bruce-Mitford, Miranda. *The Illustrated Book of Signs and Symbols* (DK Publishing, 2004). Verbally and visually, this book provides a look at and an explanation of the signs and symbols that have developed in the world over hundreds of years. All ages.

For Teachers

McNichol, Andrea, with Jeffrey A. Nelson. *Handwriting Analysis: Putting It to Work for You* (Contemporary Books, 1994). A guide to the science of graphology—interpreting handwriting.

What Your Handwriting Tells You

Look at your recent schoolwork, or write a sentence here:

It takes training to fully understand what people's handwriting says about them. It's still fun to try to guess what our writing says about us. Do any of these styles and traits fit you?

Writing Style	Personal Traits
Size	
Small	Intellectual
Large	Very active
Form	
Rounded letters	Even-tempered, well-rounded
Stiff angles	Energetic, impatient, with qualities of leadership
Slants	
Straight up and down	Able to keep cool
Forward (right)	Emotional, but able to use good judgment
Backward (left)	Quiet, timid, with a wish to live in the past
Loops	
Looped "d" or "t"	Sensitive to criticism
No loops on "d" or "t"	Emotional
Slender loops on "g," "j," or "y"	Choosy about activities and friends
Crossed "t"	
Long cross	Enthusiastic
Cross above the "t" stem	Forward-looking and imaginative
Cross misses the "t" stem on the right	Easily angered
Open "a" and "o"	
Open "mouth" on "o"	Talkative
Other open letters	Confident, open-minded, outspoken
Some letters open, some closed	Able to keep a secret
Endings	
Curved up	Generous
Abrupt or sudden	Ruled by the head rather than the heart
Curved down	Pessimistic

Learning from Mistakes

"A stumble may prevent a fall."
English proverb

Mistakes happen to everyone. Often, they offer the opportunity to learn something—different ways to act, steps to follow in completing a task, or new and creative ways to deal with a variety of situations. Let's look at some of the ways mistakes can open our eyes and our minds.

What If?

When you make a mistake, what can you do about it? In small groups, talk about ways to deal with mistakes like these:

- On the school bus, you look at your feet and see that the shoes you put on are from two different pairs.
- You get to class and realize you completed the wrong pages in your math book.
- Instead of mailing in his or her tax forms, your teacher accidentally mailed the tests you and your classmates just took.
- Arriving at what you thought was a costume party, you see that no one's wearing a costume except you.

Sports Moves

In small groups, agree on two or three sports everyone is familiar with. Talk about what happens when players make mistakes. What penalties are written into the rules? What are some other mistakes players might make? What would happen, for example, if you gripped a hockey stick in only one hand? Threw a football underhand? Used a pool cue without the second hand's support? Imagine

and pantomime some of these "mistakes." Move some more by practicing correct sporting moves of interest to everyone in the group.

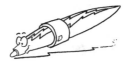

Lessons from Mistakes

Think of a mistake you've made and learned from. Write about an important lesson sparked by a mistake. If you wish, read what you've written to others in the class, or keep your writing to yourself and listen to what others have learned from their mistakes.

"I Goofed" Cards

9" x 12" sheets of construction paper • pens or fine-line markers • colored pencils or markers

Have you goofed lately and made a mistake that you regret because it affected someone else? Reach out to that person by making a simple card admitting the mistake and apologizing. Make the card on a sheet of construction paper folded in half lengthwise. It's fine to keep your message lighthearted—even humorous. You may want to illustrate the card, too. Whether you actually deliver it is up to you.

Art from Mistakes

painting paper • tempera paints or watercolors and brushes

Tip: As a variation, use pens and ink. If neither paint nor ink is available, you can draw using colored pencils or markers.

We all make mistakes. Figuring out ways to fix them—or turn them into something good—helps us see that mistakes are acceptable and can even lead us to look at things in new ways. Pour a small amount of paint on a sheet of drawing paper. Smear it a bit, as if you'd spilled by mistake. Now trade papers with someone else. What can you create out of the "mistake" your classmate made? Paint a picture. Display the finished paintings and enjoy seeing how others turned "mistakes" into works of art.

Think About It, Talk About It

- How do you feel when you make a mistake? Why?

- When you make a mistake, how can you use it as an opportunity for learning?

- What are some ways to handle very serious mistakes?

- Read the quote at the beginning of the theme. What do you think it means? Explain your answer.

Affirmation

I learn from my mistakes.

Resources

For Students

Hammond, Tim. *Sports* (Alfred A. Knopf, 2005). Take a look at the moves of the world's most popular sports while learning interesting facts and rules of the games. Ages 9–12.

Jones, Charlotte Foltz. *Mistakes That Worked* (Doubleday, 1994). Learn about mistakes that led to progress and inventions we've appreciated ever since—potato chips, silly putty, and more. Ages 9–12.

Asserting Myself

"You must learn to say no when something is not right for you."

Leontyne Price, U.S. opera singer

Being assertive means speaking up for yourself in a positive way. Learning to be assertive can help you in school, at home, with friends, in sports and other activities—and in your future life. Let's practice speaking up and speaking out.

Note: Do the third and fourth "Asserting Myself" activities in sequence.

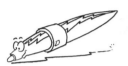

Kids' Bill of Rights

copies of handout on page 135

Do you have the right to limit the time you practice music each day? Should you have a say in your amount of daily homework? Think of the rights you'd like to include in a "Kids' Bill of Rights." Jot down a few ideas. Then, with a partner, write your own bill of rights on the handout. Are your rights sensible, to be taken seriously? Are they silly and just for laughs? It's up to you! Sign your "John Hancocks" and make it official. Post the handouts for all to see and compare. Are any of the rights similar?

Impromptu Talks

3" x 5" file cards

Think of the things you've done in school in the past few weeks. List three of these topics on a file card (examples: book title, science concept, field trip). Then choose one topic to give an unprepared one- or two-minute talk about. Form small groups for presenting and listening to the talks. Don't be shy—volunteer to speak. The topic idea is a starting point, but you can use it in any way you like. For example, for the topic of Abraham Lincoln, you might give a brief biography, take on

the role of President Lincoln discussing his political views, or pretend to be Abe Lincoln walking through the Lincoln Memorial today.

Debate Prep

a list of debate topics • a coin

Teacher: Prior to this activity, write a list of debate topics on the board. The topics should readily lend themselves to debating both "yes" and "no" positions. (Examples: Did the Louisiana Purchase benefit the people of North America? Should all coins be eliminated? Should boys and girls play together on the same teams?) *Students:* Here's a chance to work as a team to debate ideas that are important to you. Form groups of three or four—you'll need an even number of groups. Work with your teacher and other teams to choose a topic your group finds interesting. Your goal is to have two groups per topic. Flip a coin: "Heads" means your group argues the "yes" point of view, "tails" means you argue "no." Spend time agreeing how best to explain or argue that point of view. Also decide who will argue (this might be one person, two people one at a time, or each of you). You'll have 90 seconds to argue your team's side. Hang onto your notes and plans for one more activity—the actual debate.

Debates

a coin • notes from preceding activity • timer, stopwatch, or clock with a second hand

One topic at a time, hold your debate. For each topic, flip a coin to see which team presents its side first. Remember, each side has exactly 90 seconds to present its argument. Refer to your notes from the preceding activity, and follow your team's debate plan. After both sides have spoken, poll the class to see which argument was more convincing. Continue until each pair of teams has debated. What did you learn from this experience? Did being prepared help you speak up and speak out?

I Like/I Will

drawing paper • colored pencils, markers, pens and ink, or fine-line markers

Make a simple, positive reminder for yourself. Use one of these ideas, or make up your own:

- a nice thing you'll do for yourself
- an adult you trust and like to talk to
- something you like to do for fun

Keep your statement simple. (Examples: "I will take a warm bath." "I will learn a new song." "I like talking to my dad.") Personalize your statement by drawing the words in your own unique style. Make the letters wide and add a simple pattern, create curled letter ends, or color in the background behind the words. When you're finished, keep your statement handy and do the good deed for yourself.

Think About It, Talk About It

- What are some ways to calm yourself when you feel nervous, stressed, or scared? What can you say to yourself? What else can you do?

- What's the difference between being assertive and being rude or bossy? Give some examples.

Affirmation

I will speak up and speak out in positive ways.

Resources

For Students

Kaufman, Gershen, Lev Raphael, and Pamela Espeland. *Stick Up for Yourself! Every Kid's Guide to Personal Power and Positive Self-Esteem* (Free Spirit Publishing, 1999). A guide to feeling good about yourself and attaining personal power. Ages 8–12.

Otfinoski, Steven. *Speaking Up, Speaking Out* (Millbrook, 1996). Learn how to make speeches, oral reports, and social conversation and discover ways to overcome stage fright. Ages 11 and up.

For Teachers

Kaufman, Gershen, Lev Raphael, and Pamela Espeland. *A Teacher's Guide to Stick Up for Yourself!* (Free Spirit Publishing, 2000). A step-by-step curriculum that reinforces and expands the messages of the student book.

Smith, John. *Creative Calligraphy* (Anness Publishing Limited, 1998). Demonstrates techniques for making beautifully drawn letters, words, and phrases.

Kids' Bill of Rights

As kids, we believe that we should have the right to:

Signed _____ and _____

Date _____

Solving Problems

"A problem is a chance for you to do your best."

Duke Ellington (1899–1974), U.S. composer, conductor, and jazz musician

Very few days go by without a problem of some sort. Though you may wish problems would just go away, you'll be better off learning to deal with them. Put your heads together to find ways to solve problems constructively and creatively.

Note: Do the first two "Solving Problems" activities in sequence.

Problem-Solving Guidelines

chart paper • marker

When people have a problem getting along, it can help to have a general plan to follow in trying to solve it. As a class, decide on a set of guidelines to follow in handling problems at school. Start by writing ideas on the board. Once you have the guidelines clearly in mind, write them on chart paper and post the chart for future reference.

Group Problem-Solving

chart from preceding activity

Teacher: Write some or all of these problems on the board, or write some that pertain specifically to your group:

- Your best friend is becoming friends with someone else.
- You know your friend is cheating.
- Your school supplies are missing from your desk.
- The other kids think you're the teacher's pet.
- You want to be popular, but the popular kids don't seem to like you or are different from you.
- Your teacher calls on you when your hand isn't raised.

Students: Form small groups. Choose one of the problems on the board and work together to agree on a solution to try. Use the guidelines on your class chart. After ten minutes, report back to the larger group. Were you able to agree on a solution? If so, what? If not, what ideas do others in the class have to offer?

Dream Catchers

copies of handout on page 138 • colored pencils or markers • scissors • yarn • glue and feathers, ribbon, stones, shells, beads, or other decorative objects

Tip: If time permits, make dream catchers out of bent twigs or embroidery hoops with yarn for the web. (See page 137 for information on the book and craft kit *Dream Catchers* by Sylvia Tso and Donald Tso.)

Many people believe that dreams help us solve problems. Native Americans make web-like *dream catchers*. Their purpose is to catch bad dreams so they can be devoured by the spider-spirit in the web, represented by a bead or another ornament. Complete the dream catcher on the handout. Draw or glue a bead somewhere near the middle to represent the spider. Cut out your dream catcher and thread yarn through the top hole. If you wish, hang other decorative items from the bottom holes. Hang your finished dream catcher near your bed to catch your own bad dreams.

Think About It, Talk About It

- When you have a problem, should you worry, ask for help, or try to solve it on your own? What are a few good ways to tackle a problem?

- What can you do when you have a problem at school or at home that you think is too big for you to handle on your own?

- Some people believe that their dreams can help them understand and deal with problems in their lives. Do you agree? Give examples.

Creative Exercise

It's time to get moving. To do each exercise, you'll have to look for creative ways to solve the problem of not having traditional equipment or space. Here are the exercises:

- Lift weights using two items of equal weight.
- Jump rope with no rope.
- Play catch without a ball.
- Do sit-ups standing up.
- Sit in your chair and ride a bicycle.

Affirmation

I can solve problems.

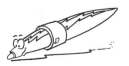

Crossword Puzzle

copies of handout on page 139

Solving problems is the subject of the crossword puzzle on the handout. Solve the puzzle on your own, or team up with a partner. *Solution:*

Resources

For Students

Tso, Sylvia, and Donald Tso, illustrations by Pamela Johnson. *Dream Catchers* (Watermill Press, 2000). A book and craft kit to create a dream catcher and learn about the importance dream catchers have played in Native American cultures. Ages 9–12.

Life Skills 137

Dream Catcher

The web of a dream catcher follows a set pattern. To follow that pattern, create your web according to the numbered example.

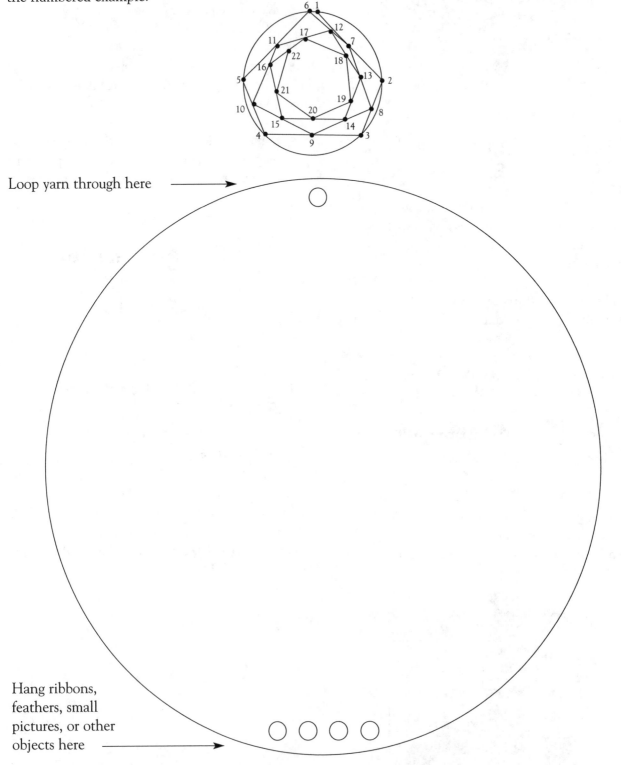

Loop yarn through here ———→

Hang ribbons, feathers, small pictures, or other objects here ———→

Problem-Solving Crossword Puzzle

The crossword puzzle's solutions all relate to solving problems. Working alone or with a partner, fill in the squares to solve this game. (The answers are on page 137.)

Across

1. These occur when you sleep
2. Done without anger or excitement
5. Attempt
6. Older folks who can sometimes help with a problem
10. A set of steps or ways to solve a problem
11. Or _____ (an alternative)
12. You and I
15. Important ingredient in getting along with others
16. Not me, but _____
17. Talk

Down

1. Bird that stands for peace
2. Clever, different, or new
3. Not found
4. Share ideas without judging
7. Hear what someone is saying
8. Special approaches; tips
9. Get along
12. Feel anxious or concerned
13. Inquire
14. Support or guidance from someone

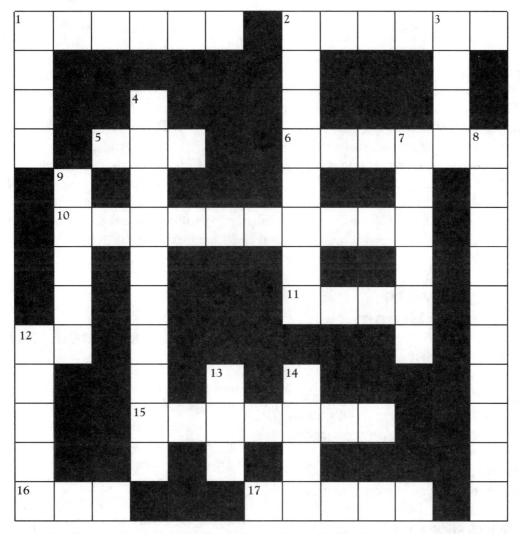

Managing Stress

Stress can come from any kind of excitement, but usually it refers to bad or bothersome feelings of tension and pressure. Since life is full of pressures both large and small, learning to manage stress is an important skill. Let's find ways to recognize stress when it's happening and discover some simple strategies for keeping it from getting out of control.

"Stress Buster" Tips

slips of paper (approx. 8½" x 2") • large envelope labeled "Stress Busters"

When it comes to dealing with stress, what works for you? On a slip of paper, write one tip for relaxing or handling stress. Don't sign your name. Place your tip in the envelope. One at a time, draw tips from the envelope and discuss the "Stress Busters." Does what works for one person always work for someone else? Are there tips that you might put to use? If there are, make a note of them. Try them when you need to ease some of the stress in your life.

Blowing Off Steam

straws in individual paper wrappers (available from food service suppliers)

Sometimes you just need a wild and crazy release. Why not blow off steam in a creative, silly, and harmless way? Take a straw in a paper wrapper. Carefully tear off one end of the wrapper. Aim for the ceiling and fire in one big blow. Watch where yours goes. Go get the wrapper, reinsert your straw, and blow again. Try making your wrapper hit a target, stick it to a wall, or cross a line.

Artful Scribbles

pencils • blank paper • colored pencils or markers (optional)

Part of managing stress is learning to deal with daily pressure by slowing down and using strategies that relax you. Here's one that's a variation on doodling: With a pencil (or two), begin scribbling briskly on a sheet of paper in any pattern that you wish. Continue scribbling while you gradually slow your hand and pencil down until you reach a stop. Fill in some of the spaces with shading, patterns, or color. Do this in a light, relaxed manner. Use this technique to ease tension when you're studying.

Biofeedback

You may not be aware of it, but your body sends you messages when you're feeling tense. Think about a stressful situation (examples: a dreaded test, an attempt to make a new friend, the scary feeling you get when watching a frightening movie or riding a wild ride at an amusement park). What happens to your body in that situation? Close your eyes and try to recall the feeling. Does your heart start to pound? Do your hands sweat? Do you feel the beginnings of a headache?

Being aware of your body's signals means that you're listening to *biofeedback*—the messages your body sends you. That feeling you get on the roller coaster may be similar to one that starts when you're worried about getting a paper turned in on time. To ease that feeling when it starts, use one of the stress-relieving activities you've learned in this theme.

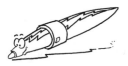

Haiku Poems

copies of handout on page 142

Haiku is a Japanese poem form. It has three non-rhyming lines: the first line has five syllables, the second has seven, and the third has five. Use the handout to write a haiku poem that tells about something that you find stressful or that guides you to relax. Before writing, you might want to work with the rest of the class to brainstorm words that suggest calmness and relaxation. You can use the words as part of your haiku.

Think About It, Talk About It

- When you're feeling overwhelmed, can thinking positively help you manage a stressful situation? How?

- Think about music, everyday sounds, and the ways people whisper, speak, or shout. How can sounds and words affect your stress level? What can they tell you about other people's feelings of stress or relaxation?

- Can stress ever be a good thing? Why or why not?

Affirmation

I can manage stress by slowing down, thinking positively, and letting off steam safely.

Resources

For Students

Leland, Nita. *The Creative Artist* (North Light Books, 1993). Discover ways to expand your creativity while learning about lines, shapes, composition, realism, abstraction, and experimentation. You'll find an example of free scribble drawing on page 102. All ages.

For Teachers

Simic, Marjorie R., Melinda McClain, and Michael Shermis. *The Confident Learner* (Grayson Bernard Publishers, 1992). This guide for parents to help a child develop a positive attitude, build self-discipline, and learn to manage stress has lots of good insights for teachers as well.

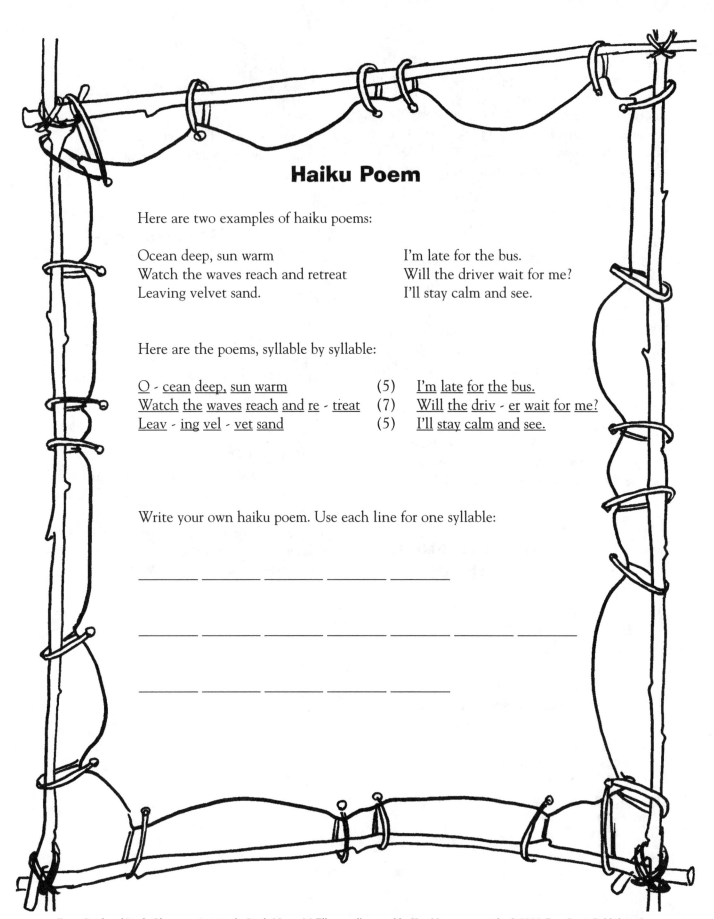

Haiku Poem

Here are two examples of haiku poems:

Ocean deep, sun warm
Watch the waves reach and retreat
Leaving velvet sand.

I'm late for the bus.
Will the driver wait for me?
I'll stay calm and see.

Here are the poems, syllable by syllable:

O - cean deep, sun warm   (5)
Watch the waves reach and re - treat   (7)
Leav - ing vel - vet sand   (5)

I'm late for the bus.
Will the driv - er wait for me?
I'll stay calm and see.

Write your own haiku poem. Use each line for one syllable:

_____ _____ _____ _____ _____

_____ _____ _____ _____ _____ _____ _____

_____ _____ _____ _____ _____

Handling Teasing

"When angry, count to ten before you speak; if very angry, a hundred."
Thomas Jefferson, third U.S. President

The best defenses against teasing are common sense and self-esteem. Let's look together for some safe and smart ways to respond to teasing. At the same time, we'll talk about the tendency to tease and how to break the habit of hurtful teasing.

Note: Do the "Handling Teasing" activities in sequence.

Talking About Teasing

chart paper • marker

Tip: There may be times when you'll need an adult's help in handling or putting a stop to teasing.

What can you do when someone teases you? When you're with someone who's teasing another person? Talk about ways to handle teasing and what might happen from using different responses. Come up with a list of ways to deal with teasing. Post the list as a reminder that there are lots of ways to avoid giving in to teasing.

Showing How It Feels

scarves, bandannas, or paper bags

Divide into two groups. While one group watches, the other group can demonstrate how it feels to be teased. The actors should cover their faces and use only body movements to show this feeling. Reverse roles. While the first acting group observes, the second group, with faces covered, can pantomime movements and postures for dealing with teasing effectively and safely. What do these unspoken messages communicate?

Shield Designs

copies of handout on page 145 • colored pencils or markers

You don't have to let teasing bring on tears or lead to fighting. Think of yourself armored with a protective shield—a positive self-image and the ability to walk away. On the handout, design a shield that shows or tells what will help you protect yourself from teasing. You might write words (examples: "Don't fight back," "Walk away"), draw a picture, or use colors and patterns that show your calm confidence. The next time someone teases you, picture your "tease-proof" shield in your mind and remember that you don't need to give in to teasing.

Anti-Teasing Code

posterboard • markers

Sometimes we tease people without thinking about how they might feel. Fight the teasing habit by developing an "anti-teasing" code. In small groups, come up with some ideas or guidelines that might help you and others remember not to tease. Turn your list into a poster that's colorful and eye-catching. Save the posters for one more activity.

Sharing the Code

posters from preceding activity

Teachers: Ahead of time, arrange for students to go into a classroom of younger children to share their posters and discuss teasing. *Students:* In your small groups from the previous activity, visit a class of younger students. Bring your poster. Explain your anti-teasing code and the reasons for it. Invite children to suggest ideas for handling teasing and for breaking the "teasing habit."

Think About It, Talk About It

- Why do you think people tease?

- Have you ever teased someone and later wished you hadn't? Why did you decide to tease? What made you feel bad later? What did you do about it? Did that help?

- Do you think it's wise to let teasing get the best of you? Should you show your fears or tears? Why not?

- What kind of body language will help you or hurt you in a confrontation with someone who teases you?

- Can teasing ever be fun for both the teaser and the person being teased? If so, how can you know it's okay to tease? Explain your answer.

Affirmation

I can handle teasing by being sure of myself and planning the right thing to do. I don't need to tease others to feel good about myself.

Resources

For Students

Polocco, Patricia. *Thank You, Mr. Falker* (Philomel Books, 1998). An autobiographical story tells of how the author was tormented by teasing as a child and how a compassionate teacher helped everyone involved. Ages 8–10.

Romain, Trevor. *Bullies Are a Pain in the Brain* (Free Spirit Publishing, 1997). A short, humorous guide that teaches kids how to be bully-proof and how to stop being teased or threatened. Includes resources and advice for teachers and parents. Ages 8–12.

Tease-Proof Shield

Taking Care of Myself

"Health is number one. You can't have a good offense, a good defense, good education, or anything else if you don't have good health."

Sarah McClendon, U.S. journalist

Eating right, exercising, and tending to your emotional well-being help you feel good about yourself. Take charge of your health. It's one of the most important things you can do for yourself—now and for the future.

Healthy Moves

radio or CD or tape player with favorite music for movement (optional)

Give the day a healthy start—or take an energizing break—with a low-key workout of warm-ups, stretches, and a cooldown. If you want, add music with an easy, steady beat. Take turns leading the class in your own favorite movements, or make up moves as you go.

Food Pyramids from Around the Globe

copies of handout on page 148 • colored pencils or markers

Are you putting a balance of foods into your body to keep it strong and healthy? People from different areas around the world balance their food and nutrition needs differently. Look at all of the food pyramids on your handout. Use a colored pencil or marker and outline or color all of the similar food groups in the different pyramids in the same color. (For example, you could use green to highlight vegetables in all of the pyramids.) After you've finished, list a food suggestion that is unique to each culture. Ask yourself, what makes a particular culture's food recommendation *different?* In the inner circle, list a couple of healthy food recommendations that are *common* to all cultures. What do all of the Food Pyramids have in common? After looking at the different pyramids, are you interested in trying any foods that are new to you?

Personal Food Pyramids

copies of handouts on pages 148 and 149 • colored pencils or markers

Plan a day's worth of healthy foods that fit the guidelines *and* your own taste buds. Look at the different food pyramids that show healthy balances of types of foods. Fill in the blank food pyramid with writing or pictures showing your own personalized food plan. Take your pyramid home and share your healthy eating plan with your family.

Good Words

Good words help you feel healthy, so join your classmates in boosting everyone's mental health. Write your name across the top of a sheet of paper while your classmates do the same. Pass the papers around and write positive comments about the owner of each page that comes your way. Be sincere, simple, and creative. (Examples: "Thanks for being so cheerful first hour." "Nice smile!"

"Way to go on that science project!") Sign your comment only if you want to. When your paper comes back to you, bask in the good words.

Personal Health Plan

copies of handout on page 150

You know that you need the right foods, regular exercise, and a balance of work and relaxation to stay healthy. Use the handout to plan a day that's healthy for your mind and body from beginning to end. If you like, ask your teacher for extra copies of the handout so you can plan other healthy days, too. Share your plan with an adult in your family and ask for support in your commitment to take care of yourself. Here's to your health!

Think About It, Talk About It

- Besides a balance of good diet, sleep, exercise, work, and relaxation, what are other ways to take care of yourself? (Examples: wearing a seat belt in the car, watching out for traffic as you cross a street.)

- Why are sleep and a good breakfast important in the long run? In the short run?

- Some people have trouble eating first thing in the morning. Share some tips for fueling your body at the beginning of the day.

- Think about the foods advertised in magazines, TV commercials, and the grocery store. How is your diet influenced by advertising? Is this good or bad? Why?

- What people and activities boost your mental health? How? Be specific.

- Does watching TV or playing computer or video games keep you from getting exercise? How can you find a balance?

Affirmation

I will stay healthy by being good to myself physically and emotionally.

Resources

For Students

Sadgrove, Judy. *Exercise* (Raintree Steck-Vaughn Company, 2000). Learn about the physical and psychological effects of exercise and the benefits and risks of solo and group sports. This book may help you find the sport that's perfect for you. Also includes warm-ups and stretching exercises.

Stromoski, Rick. *Food Rules! The Stuff You Munch, Its Crunch, Its Punch, and Why You Sometimes Lose Your Lunch* (Puffin Books, 2001). This amusing and illustrated book includes fascinating facts and information that comprehensively cover food and nutrition.

For Teachers

Oldways: The Food Issues Think Tank. The Oldways Preservation and Exchange Trust is a nonprofit organization that translates the complex details of nutrition science into everyday language and good advice. Visit their site at www.oldwayspt.org to download free copies of four healthy eating pyramids based on Asian, Latin American, Mediterranean, and vegetarian diets. Versions are available for adults and children.

Willett, Walter C., M.D. *Eat, Drink, and Be Healthy: The Harvard Medical School Guide to Healthy Eating* (Simon and Schuster, 2001). This book describes an alternative to the USDA's Food Guide Pyramid. Created by experts at the Harvard School of Public Health, it's called the Healthy Eating Pyramid.

Food Pyramids from Around the Globe

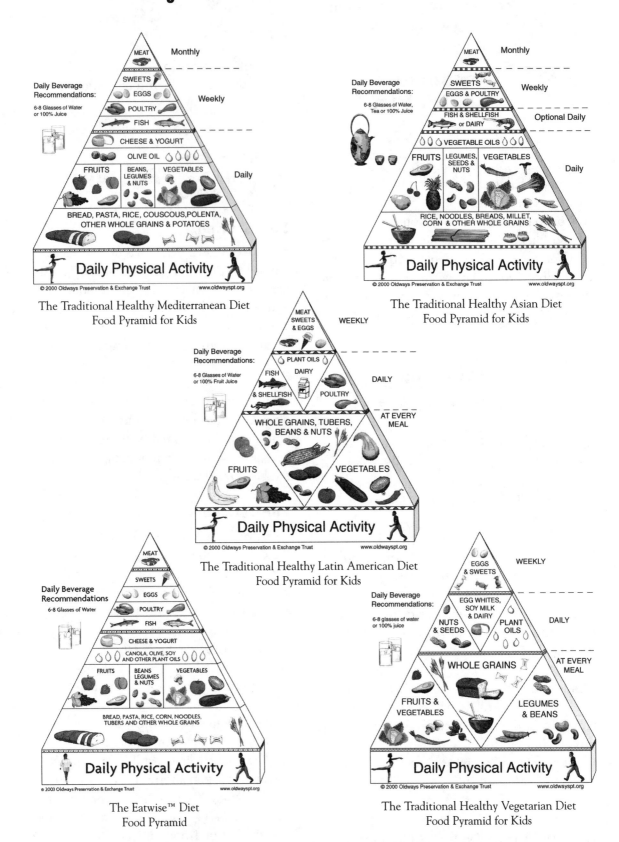

The Traditional Healthy Mediterranean Diet
Food Pyramid for Kids

The Traditional Healthy Asian Diet
Food Pyramid for Kids

The Traditional Healthy Latin American Diet
Food Pyramid for Kids

The Eatwise™ Diet
Food Pyramid

The Traditional Healthy Vegetarian Diet
Food Pyramid for Kids

My Personal Pyramid

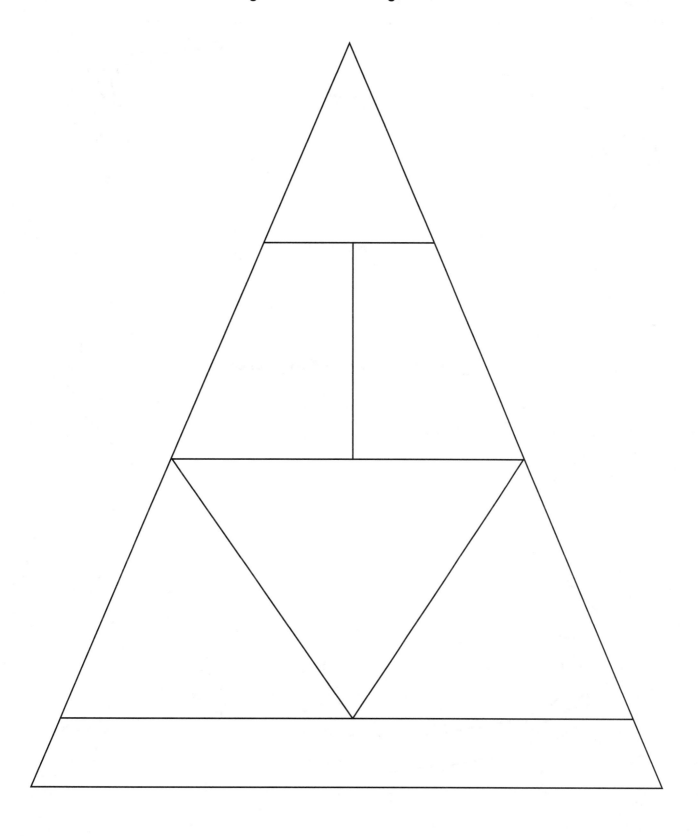

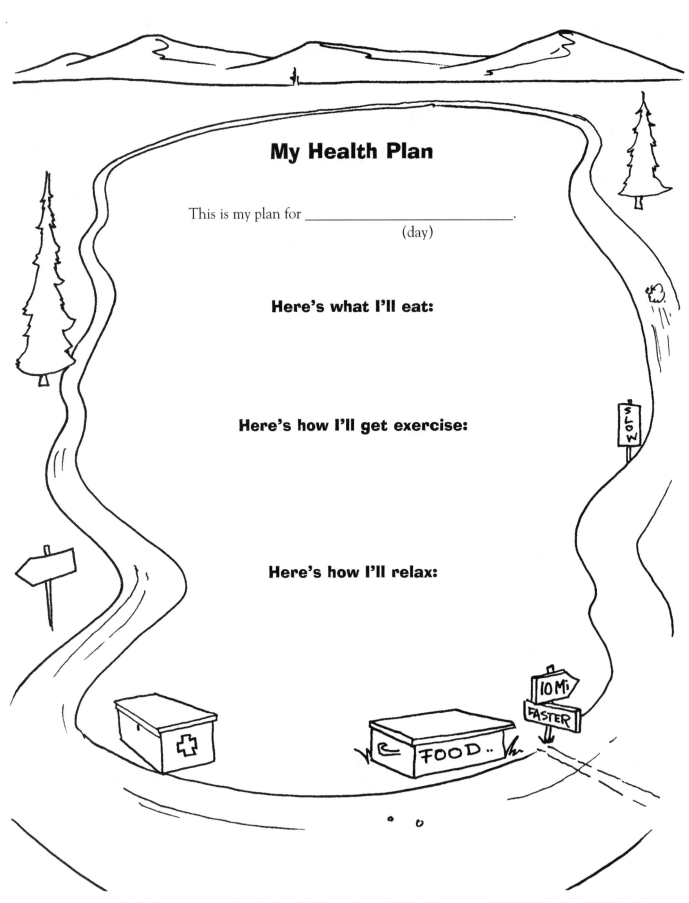

My Health Plan

This is my plan for _____.
(day)

Here's what I'll eat:

Here's how I'll get exercise:

Here's how I'll relax:

Using My Imagination

"All acts performed in the world begin in the imagination."

Barbara Grizzuti Harrison, U.S. writer

Music, dance, art, science, exploration, invention—all of culture springs from imagination. Within you is a well of creativity. To be fully you, it's important that you reach into that well, draw out your imaginative force, and use it! Get ready to tap your creativity as you explore new ways to think about the world and your place in it. You'll travel across time and geography to take on some new and different roles.

 ## Storytelling

A Chinese legend tells how four creatures helped P'an Ku create the world. The dragon of the east brought the spring rain. The phoenix, a bird from the south, brought the dry summer weather. The tiger of the west used his powers to turn summer's greenery into the golds, reds, and browns of autumn. The tortoise, a creature from the north, supported the winter sky. Upon P'an Ku's death, this creator's blood became rivers, his sweat became rain, his flesh soil, his breath wind, and his voice thunder. What happened to the four creatures? Did the tortoise remain to keep the earth and sky from meeting? Did the dragon miss its friend P'an Ku and weep till the rain became a flood? Divide into four groups and create your own story about one of the different creatures. After 10–15 minutes, share your stories with the class.

 ## Cave Pictures

smooth rocks or sheets of gray construction paper cut in the shape of rocks • permanent markers

Tip: Bring in a few extra rocks to make sure there will be enough to go around.

Teacher: Ahead of time, ask each student to find and bring in a smooth rock large enough to draw a small picture on. *Students:* Your ancestors used Earth's natural paints—ochre and charcoal—to draw stories about their lives on cave walls and to leave their handprints. Just as these cave dwellers did 18,000 years ago, draw a picture that tells about you and your world. Since you don't live in a cave, draw or write your message on a smooth rock. When it's complete, remember to sign your work, cave-dweller style, but using your thumb instead of your hand. Use the marker to color the bottom of your thumb, then press it to the rock. This artifact can tell your story to future generations.

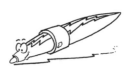 ## Hieroglyphics

copies of handouts on pages 154 and 155

The ancient Egyptian writing system was called *hieroglyphics*. Decipher the hieroglyphics that might have been found in an Egyptian tomb. Look at the

Hieroglyphic Message handout. Work with a partner to solve this puzzle. (Note that many sounds have more than one symbol.) When you're finished, take some time to represent your own name using hieroglyphic pictures. Later, stretch your imagination by writing more with hieroglyphs or by inventing your own alphabet or writing system. *Solution:* Cats are sacred and (n) become mummies.

Pony Express Riders

Travel back in time a mere 140 years and imagine yourself riding the plains, cliffs, and mountains from Missouri to California as a Pony Express rider. Grab the imaginary reigns in front of you as you sit high in the saddle (your desk chair). Mime your journey to deliver the mail with actions only—no words. The ride is rough, tough, and dangerous, and you have to go fast and steady. Try to use your eyes, sway your shoulders, move your hips and arms, and use those reins. Take turns calling out a route. Example: "This mesa is high and flat, but soon you find yourself on a narrow path heading up a rocky ledge . . . Now you're battling rushing waters . . . Watch out—bandits ahead! Can you outsmart them? . . . Success! You've arrived at your destination and safely delivered the mail." After your ride, dismount your "horse," stand up, and give your saddle-sore body a stretch.

Imagining Ways to Help the World

Imagine yourself working to make the world a better place. What's your cause? Saving the rain forests? A multinational space station? Racial harmony? A peaceful world? Form groups with others who share your special interest. Talk about ways to be involved. Use the resources on this page, or share ideas for learning more about how kids can make a difference. If this discussion sparks your enthusiasm, follow through in setting and following your own plan for helping the world.

Think About It, Talk About It

- What are some ways the world has changed since the time of the cave dwellers? Since ancient times? Since a century ago? What are some ways it hasn't changed?

- How do you think imagination has helped the world? How has it hurt the world?

- Are there ways you can practice or exercise your imagination? Explain your ideas.

Affirmation

My imagination gives me new ways to look at the world and grow.

Resources

For Students

Lewis, Barbara. *The Kid's Guide to Social Action: How to Solve the Social Problems You Choose—and Turn Creative Thinking into Positive Action* (Revised, Expanded, Updated Edition) (Free Spirit Publishing, 1998). Shows kids ways to tackle social problems through positive action. Ages 10 and up.

Philip, Neil, illustrations by Nilesh Mistry. *The Illustrated Book of Myths: Tales and Legends of the World* (Dorling Lindersley Ltd., 1995). Offers fascinating glimpses into various cultures. Ages 9–12.

Hieroglyphic Alphabet

Hieroglyphic Message

Clues

1. Hieroglyphs represent sounds. That means the hieroglyph for the letter "c" could have a hard sound, as in "cake," or a soft sound, as in "circus."
2. Because it represents a sound, a single hieroglyph may be used to represent a group of English letters. For example, the hieroglyph for "b" sounds like "be" and can be used to represent the word "be." In the same way, the hieroglyph for "r" can mean "are" and the hieroglyph for "u" can mean "you."
3. Some symbols have the sound of more than one English letter. Some English letters have more than one symbol.
4. Some sounds may not be represented. That's where your own imagination comes in!

Use the hieroglyphic alphabet, the clues above, and your imagination to decode this message:

Write your own name, or a message about yourself, using hieroglyphics:

Inventing

"It is kind of fun to do the impossible."

Walt Disney (1901–1966), U.S. movie animator and producer

Inventions come from using the imagination to think differently. Scientists, clothing designers, architects, sociologists, computer wizards—and kids like you—have all contributed to inventions that have changed our world. Here's a chance for you to try your own skills at inventing by recognizing or predicting future needs and imagining ways to meet them.

Computerized Clothing

drawing paper • drawing pencils, colored pencils, or markers

Imagine you are competing to design the newest trend in clothing—wearable computers. The clothing must have one or more computer gadgets woven into the fabric (examples: laptops, MP3 player, phone, blood-pressure monitor, or video camera). The world is looking to you to make a smart garment. Create yours on paper, then share your designs with your classmates.

Robot Moves

hula hoops (optional)

Futurists tell us that robots will play an ever-larger role in our lives. Take a break and reinvent yourself as a robot. Exaggerate your walk, talk, and movements. Practice going around the room as if you were on a runway in front of a crowd of spectators. The cameras are flashing and you are pretty dashing! Show off your mechanics with rigid jerks or with smooth, fluid electronic movements. To add to the fun, use a hula hoop robot-style.

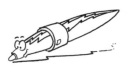

Toys of the Future

chart paper and marker • drawing paper and pencils

Think of the toys you played with when you were younger or may still enjoy today: LEGOs, action figures, Beanie Babies—the list is endless. Some toys have changed over the years. For example, a clever inventor combined the scooter of yesteryear with a surfboard to create the skateboard. Every toy began in an inventive person's mind. As a group, list some toy fads of the past and present. Look at your list and think of toys kids of the future might enjoy. Then sketch a picture and write a description of your idea for a terrific future toy or a new twist on an old one.

Ranking Inventions

copies of handout on page 158

One hundred years ago, many of the appliances, medicines, and conveniences we take for granted didn't exist or were just being introduced. In small groups, read the list of items on the handout. How important is each item in your life? Are there any you could live without? Rank them from most to least important. Then guess when each item was invented. (Some go back more than a hundred years.) Did all of the groups agree? Is there something missing from the list that *you* can't do without? *Solution:* personal computer, 1975; zipper with fastener, 1913; DVD player, 1996; aspirin, 1853; television, 1931; ice cream cone, 1904; submarine, 1624; basketball, 1891; automobile, 1885; telephone, 1876; Barbie doll, 1958; McDonald's restaurant, 1955; hair dryer, 1925; pencil with attached eraser, 1858; handheld video camera, 1981; lightbulb, 1879; potato chips, 1853; laser, 1960; school, 400 B.C.; Ferris wheel, 1893; hot dog bun, 1904; laptop computer, 1987; electric guitar, 1935; MP3 player, 1997; microwave oven, 1945.

Street of the Future

book or art print with an artist's rendition of a street scene (optional) • drawing paper • colored pencils or markers

Look at a painting of a street scene, or recall an image of a crowded street from TV, the movies, or your own experience. Do clues (such as architecture, vehicles, or clothing) give you hints about the street's time period? Draw a picture of a city street representing life fifty years from now. Include invented vehicles, clothes, personal items, and other gadgets that might be part of daily life.

Think About It, Talk About It

- What are the great inventions or discoveries of your lifetime?

- Have you ever talked to a parent, grandparent, or teacher and realized that something you take for granted was not invented during that grown-up's childhood? Give examples.

- Do you have a good idea for an invention or an inventive solution to a problem? Describe it.

- What is something you wish would be invented?

Affirmation

I have the ability to invent.

Resources

For Students

Erlbach, Arlene. *The Kids' Invention Book* (Lerner Publications, 1999). True stories about successful inventions by kids.

St. George, Judith, illustrations by David Small. *So You Want to Be an Inventor?* (Philomel, 2002). Stories of historical inventors are mixed with tips and inspiration to turn dreams into inventions.

25 Inventions

Here are 25 inventions from the past. Use the line on the left to rank how important each invention is to you (from 1–25, with 1 being most important). Write your guess for what year each item was invented in the right-hand boxes. The answers are on pages 156–157.

_____ personal computer ☐   _____ pencil with attached eraser ☐

_____ zipper with fastener ☐

        _____ handheld video camera ☐

_____ DVD player ☐

        _____ lightbulb ☐

_____ aspirin ☐

        _____ potato chips ☐

_____ television ☐

        _____ laser ☐

_____ ice cream cone ☐

        _____ school ☐

_____ submarine ☐

        _____ Ferris wheel ☐

_____ basketball ☐

        _____ hot dog bun ☐

_____ automobile ☐

        _____ laptop computer ☐

_____ telephone ☐

        _____ electric guitar ☐

_____ Barbie doll ☐

        _____ MP3 player ☐

_____ McDonald's restaurant ☐

        _____ microwave oven ☐

_____ hair dryer ☐

Laughing About It

"Laughter translates into any language."

Anonymous

It's fun to laugh and, as an added benefit, there's scientific evidence that laughing is good for your health and well-being. Take some time to share jokes and laughs with your classmates. There's only one rule: No jokes at someone else's expense. There's plenty of friendly humor to go around!

Note: Do the first two "Laughing About It" activities in sequence.

Funny Memory Drawings

drawing paper • colored pencils or markers

What's the funniest thing that ever happened to you? Draw a picture of this event. When you're done, display your drawing with your classmates' and share some of the stories behind the pictures. Save the drawings for one more activity.

Funny Role-Plays

drawings from preceding activity

Team up in small groups. Look at your group members' drawings and choose one laughable situation to act out. Role-play the memory as it happened, or come up with another funny turn of events. Be creative, and laugh all you want!

Sharing the "Funnies"

a variety of newspapers and magazines with humorous content

What's funny to you? Scan newspapers and magazines looking for humor. Then take things a step further by explaining what makes each humorous item funny. How are ordinary things turned into laughable commentaries? Is it through jokes, funny facial expressions, or headlines that make a play on words? Relax and enjoy swapping funny cartoons, comics, headlines, and pictures. And here's a tip: Enlighten the adults in your life about what makes you chuckle. They might discover a side of you they never knew about—and vice versa.

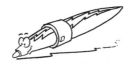

50 Excuses for Laughing

Team up and get your funny minds going by making a list of 50 excuses for laughing. Be outrageous or slaphappy if you wish. When you're done, post the ideas on the chalkboard or bulletin board and add to the lists as new ideas occur to you.

50 Excuses for Laughing

1. Shawna wiggles her ears at us
2. The teacher gives us "the eye"
3. I put my shirt on inside out
4. Oops! There's milk on my face!
5.

Prescription for Laughter

copies of handout on page 161

There's a saying, "Laughter is the best medicine." On the handout, write a prescription for what every kid needs each day to have a healthy dose of laughter. Does "Dr. You" prescribe something gross and gooey? Nonsensical? Unexpected? When you're through, pass the prescriptions around and share the laughter.

Have a good breakfast and a teacher who thinks it's funny if you scrunch up your face like Jim Carrey

Signed Dr. Michaela Brown-Valtz

Think About It, Talk About It

- What makes something funny?

- Why do you think laughter is contagious?

- Is what's funny the same for each person? Why do people laugh at different things?

- Can you tell about a time when you wanted to stop laughing but couldn't?

- Why do we sometimes want to laugh at inappropriate times?

- Who are your favorite comedians, cartoonists, or humorous writers? What makes them funny?

Affirmation

Laughter is good for me.

Resources

For Students

Prelutsky, Jack, drawings by James Stevenson. *Something Big Has Been Here* (Scholastic, 1990). A collection of humorous poetry that will spark funny bones—and funny minds. Ages 5–9.

For Teachers

The HUMOR Project. Look for a daily "Laffirmation" and have a chuckle at this Web site: www.humorproject.com

Loomans, Diane, and Karen Kolberg. *The Laughing Classroom* (HJ Kramer, 2002). An activity book that will help energize your classroom and create a learning environment of humor, playfulness, and spontaneity.

Prescription for Laughter

For a healthy dose
of daily laughter

Signed **Dr.** _____

Clowning Around

"You grow up the day you have your first real laugh at yourself."

Ethel Barrymore (1879–1959), U.S. actress

If you think clowns are for little kids, think again. Getting a laugh can be hard work. Professional clowns are adults who've taken their natural talent for making people laugh and turned it into a job. Come along to clown college and try out some ways to use your mind, body, and talent for clowning around. Remember, humor shared with others is one of the greatest gifts you can give.

Note: Do the "Clowning Around" activities in sequence.

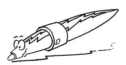

Clown College Applications

copies of handout on page 164

Your first step toward clown college is filling out the application. As you answer the questions on the handout, think about what the information says about the unique ways you can share your humor. Be truthful or daring—it's up to you! Display the applications and look for another applicant you might have fun clowning around with.

Lesson 1: Facial Expressions

completed applications from preceding activity

You've looked at your classmates' applications. Now form groups of two or three clown candidates. You will learn the art of clowning together. The first lesson is about facial expressions. Show each other how you can use just your faces to show some of these ideas:

- "That's really funny!"
- "Aha! I found him!"
- "I've got a great idea!"
- "Yes! Yes! Yeeesss!!!"
- "Would you—please?"
- "I'm so embarrassed!"

- "I'm really sad."
- "Can I trust her?"
- "I'm very confused."
- "That's not fair."
- "Now I'm mad!"
- "No! No! Noooo!!!"

Lesson 2: Adding Body Movements

Join up with your partners from Lesson 1. Use some of the same ideas from that lesson as the basis for practicing body movements. How can your body show crying? Embarrassment? Excitement? Watch each other. Is there a simple prop that would enhance your clown act? Look around for something to add zest to your clowning around. (Of course, you can always pantomime.) Put the body movements together with props and facial expressions into a short, funny routine involving each clown in your group (example: getting wet in the rain, coming indoors, and shaking out wet umbrellas). Practice one routine to get it down.

Lesson 3: "Selling" Your Act

drawing paper • colorful markers and fine-line markers

There's more to the business of clowning than funny routines. You need to find a way to advertise your act so people will be eager to see it. Join forces with your partners again, and create a flyer inviting others to come see your act. Be creative, and remember that a picture and a few words can tell a lot! Post your group's flyer next to others in preparation for one more activity.

Graduation Performance

flyers from preceding activity • box for flyers (optional)

Congratulations! You've graduated from clown college. Now your group gets to share your clown act with your fellow graduates. If everyone wants to volunteer at once, put the flyers in a box and draw to see which group will go first. Bask in the laughs of your audience and invite helpful hints. If you're on a roll, plan to carry on your clown antics for other audiences of friends or family.

Think About It, Talk About It

- What do you think a real clown college looks for in its applicants?

- Do all clowns wear costumes? Can you think of a clown, on stage or screen, who does not wear a traditional clown costume? What does this person do to earn the title of clown? Be specific.

- Do you have a silly side? What helps bring it out?

Affirmation

It's only silly me, clowning around!

Resources

For Students

Steele, H. Thomas. *1000 Clowns: More of Less* (Taschen, 2004). Learn about the international history of clowning and the "8 Clown Commandments" alongside colorful clown images.

For Teachers

Great clowns may not always be in costume. Classic acts of legendary clowns from television, such as Red Skelton, Lucille Ball, and Victor Borge, are available on video. Check your local library, media center, or video store. Contemporary clowns include Jim Carrey, Eddie Murphy, and Amanda Bynes.

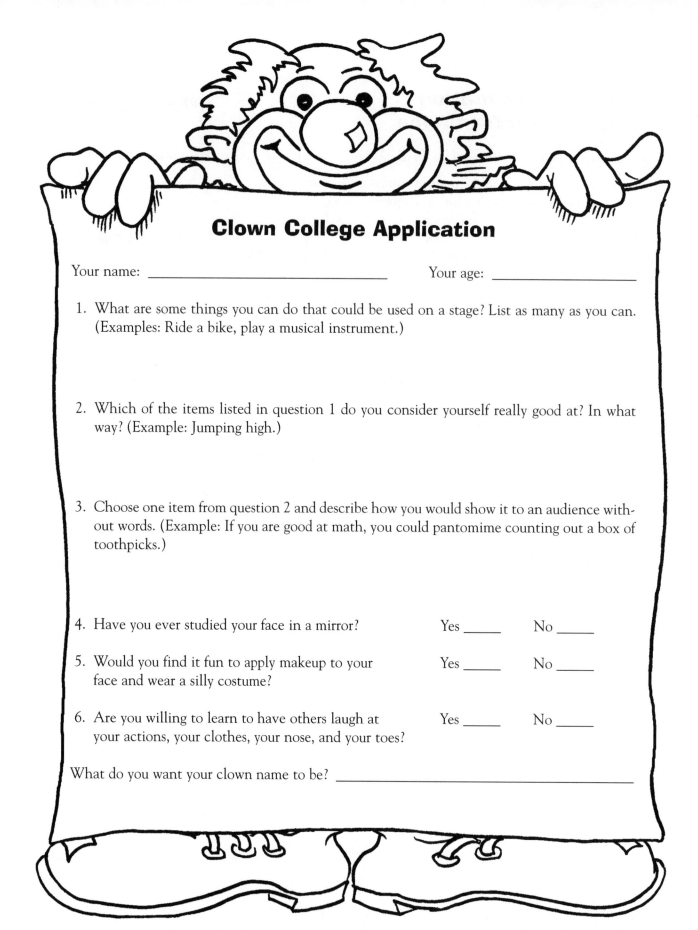

Clown College Application

Your name: _____   Your age: _____

1. What are some things you can do that could be used on a stage? List as many as you can. (Examples: Ride a bike, play a musical instrument.)

2. Which of the items listed in question 1 do you consider yourself really good at? In what way? (Example: Jumping high.)

3. Choose one item from question 2 and describe how you would show it to an audience without words. (Example: If you are good at math, you could pantomime counting out a box of toothpicks.)

4. Have you ever studied your face in a mirror?   Yes _____   No _____

5. Would you find it fun to apply makeup to your face and wear a silly costume?   Yes _____   No _____

6. Are you willing to learn to have others laugh at your actions, your clothes, your nose, and your toes?   Yes _____   No _____

What do you want your clown name to be? _____

Showing My Art and Soul

"Every child is an artist."

Pablo Picasso (1881–1973), Spanish painter and sculptor

It's hard to imagine a world without books, paintings, movies, and songs. It is through art that people express and explore their deepest feelings. You are an artist in many ways. Art is a way of expressing yourself. You might do this through writing, dancing, drawing, making music, or telling stories. Come along and discover a variety of ways to express the artistry and creativity in you.

Backpack Art

items from backpacks or desks

Tip: Use an instant or a digital camera to take pictures of the artwork.

Take out a few items from your backpack or desk (examples: erasers, paper clips, pencils, mittens, math tools, a box of raisins). Using your cleared desktop as a canvas, put the objects together to "paint" a picture. Your work of art might be abstract, or it might represent something real. When your backpack art is completed, tour the room admiring the art of others while they admire yours.

Song Lyrics

radio or CD or tape player with favorite music

What's your current favorite song? Is it a rock, rap, hip-hop, R&B, folk, country, alternative, jazz, or show song? Take the role of *lyricist*—someone who writes the words to songs—and come up with a new set of lyrics for that special tune. Change the whole song or part of it, or add a new verse. Let your song's topic focus on something you care about in your heart and soul. Compose alone or with others. When you're done, volunteer to perform your revised song or recite the new lyrics.

Class Stories

Tip: Allowing more than one class period will add depth to this activity.

Form groups of six to eight people to write a group story. Arrange your desks in a circle. Put your name at the top of a sheet of notebook paper and write a beginning sentence to a story. Pass that paper to the person on your left. You'll receive someone else's story beginning. Write the next sentence and pass that story on. When you receive the story with the name of the person on your left, you'll know you're the last author, and your task will be to write

the final sentence. When you're done, read a complete story or two aloud in your group. How do different ideas help make a story interesting? Though the group stories may not be polished, combining ideas with other people can help you expand your own thinking. If you want, follow through and rewrite one of the stories on your own.

 # Choreography

CD or tape player with music for movement (optional)

If you've ever watched a dance, play, movie, or musical, you've seen the work of choreographers. In the theater, *choreography* is the art of planning movements, dance steps, or even staged fights step-by-step. Experiment with some choreography of your own. Alone or with others, step out as a boxer in a ring, a tap dancer, an aerobics instructor, a fencer with a sword, a marching band member, or an excited Super Bowl winner. Remember to choreograph arm movements, too.

 # Custom Clothing Design

clothing and hobby catalogs (optional) • drawing paper • colored pencils or markers

What do clothes and accessories tell you about people? How can you tell, just by looking, that someone is a businessperson, diver, soldier, ceremonial dancer, carpenter, rock musician, chef, or student? Here's a chance to design the ideal outfit—clothes, accessories, and equipment—for any purpose you'd like. Page through catalogs for ideas, or come up with your own.

 # Think About It, Talk About It

- Can you express in songs, visual art, or dancing something that's hard to share otherwise? Give some examples.

- You've received a full scholarship to the art school of your choice. What *discipline* will you study—fine art, music, dance, theater, literature, film, design, or something else? Explain your choice.

- If a studio were to make a movie of your life, what actor would play you? Why?

- What do clothes and how they are worn say about the people wearing them? Explain.

- Do you think it's important to study the arts? As important as science, math, or social studies? As important as cooking or woodworking? Why or why not?

 # Affirmation

It's good for me to show my art and soul.

 # Resources

For Students

Gordon, Lynn, illustrations by Karen Johnson and Susan Synarski. *Super Duper Art and Craft Book* (Chronicle Books, 2005). Creative projects with simple supplies and recycled materials. Step-by-step instructions and fun illustrations accompany each project.

Phleger, Susanne. *A Day with Picasso* (Adventures in Art) (Prestel Publishing, 1999). Picasso's life, art, and eccentricities are all explored in this book. Ages 9–12.

Curiosity Leads to Discovery

"The only real voyage of discovery consists not in seeking new landscapes but in having new eyes."
Marcel Proust (1871–1922), French novelist

Curiosity is what makes you want to learn. It can open the door to a lifelong hobby or lead you down the path to a future career. You're about to dabble in stamps, coins, maps, sports, and nature. See what sparks your interest. If you're curious to learn more, check the resources in this book, at the library, or on the Internet.

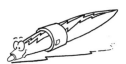

Discovering Stamps

copies of handout on page 169 • a variety of unused or canceled stamps • colored pencils or markers

Did you ever take a good look at the postage stamps on letters that come in the mail? Each stamp is a work of art that has a special story and a reason its design was chosen. The general public suggests most of the ideas for new stamps—which means that *you* can send in a suggestion. Start by making a stamp design of your own. Look at existing stamps to see what details go into them. Sketch out some ideas before drawing your design on the handout. Are you curious to learn more? Write to the Citizens' Stamp Advisory Committee (see "Resources," page 168) for guidelines on submitting stamp ideas. Maybe your idea will fly—nationwide on the fronts of envelopes!

Moving Like the Athletes

Take a good look at the sports cards you collect. Have you ever wondered how those photographs are captured? Your sports heroes *are* wonders—not only due to hard work, practice, and exercise, but also to the creativity of photographers and their crews. Some shots are staged on trampolines and in studios, with cameras ready to grab that one perfect move. The same is true out in the field. Coaches and players plan and work hard for success. One thing they do is create a kind of sports sign language for conferring across a field or an arena. Get up and practice some of the common sports signals. Who knows how to say "Out!" in baseball, or "Start the clock" for football? Try other signals that you know, or come up with your own signals to share.

Discovering Coins

a variety of coins and currency from your own or other countries • drawing paper • colored pencils or markers

Somewhere deep in your pocket, desk, or backpack there's a miniature work of art—a coin. A lot goes into a coin's creation. First, its image and words must be designed, engraved, and sculpted by an artist. Depending on its country, the coin must include certain images and words as well. U.S. coins, for example, need to show someone's profile, a date, the coin's amount, and the words "United States of America," "Liberty," and "E Pluribus Unum" (meaning "one out of many"). Design and draw your own version of a new coin or currency bill. Before you begin, take a look at some coins and bills and see what's needed for a particular country's money.

Exploring Maps

a variety of maps • paper for map designing • pencils with erasers • fine-line markers

Mapping is a process that changes as the places on the maps change. In small groups, explore different maps: a contour map, an aerial map, a park trails map, a globe. Then look at a map of your community. Find your home, school, police and fire departments, hospital, government center, museums, and points of interest. Now it's your turn to be the mapmaker. Your map might be a picture of the route from your home to school, a contour drawing of hills or desert land you like to explore, or a map of the inside of your school. Look at the samples as you work on your drawing. When you're done, photocopy your map so others can use it.

Nature Dioramas

small objects from nature • various small boxes • glue or tape • drawing paper • colored pencils or markers • scissors

Tip: Bring in a few extra objects in case someone doesn't have one.

Teacher: In advance, ask students to bring in a natural object, small enough to display in a box. *Students:* What objects in nature interest you? Butterflies who journey nearly 4,000 miles each year as they migrate? Leaves that appear in the spring, grow in the summer, and change color in the fall? Rocks left by glaciers hundreds of thousands of years ago? Mount a simple display to showcase this interest. First, glue or tape your object (or a picture of it that you've drawn) in the foreground of the box. Add illustrations, words, or details to enhance your display. If you like, make other dioramas at home and create your own museum.

Think About It, Talk About It

- Today is your lucky day: your teacher will let you spend the entire morning working on something you're curious about. What will you work on? What do you want to learn?

- Has curiosity about something led you to become an avid learner or an expert? Describe how your curiosity sparked your interest.

- Do you collect anything? How does collecting lead you to discover more about something that interests you?

Affirmation

I can explore what I'm curious about and enjoy learning something new.

Resources

For Students

United States Mint. The kids' section at the U.S. Mint's Web site is full of information on money, interactive games, and more. Web site: www.usmint.gov/kids

For Teachers

U.S. Postal Service Citizens' Stamp Advisory Committee. To receive a booklet on general guidelines for stamp proposals, write to this organization: Citizens' Stamp Advisory Committee, U.S. Postal Service Stamp Development, Room 5670, 475 L'Enfant Plaza SW, Washington, DC 20260-2437.

Stamp Design

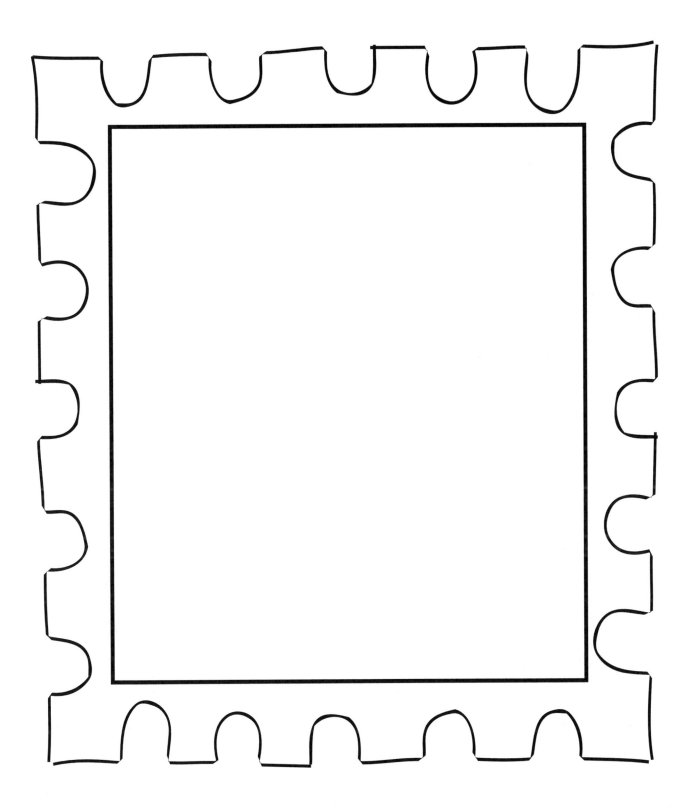

Index

About the Author

Linda Nason McElherne, M.A., is an educator, designer, artist, and national presenter. As a teacher of elementary and middle school students, she developed an enrichment program called "Arts Awareness" to help classroom teachers integrate the arts into their curriculum. Her latest efforts are bringing architecture/design and global art exchange programs to students of all ages. Linda is a mother of four and lives in Hinsdale, Illinois.

OTHER GREAT BOOKS FROM FREE SPIRIT

What Do You Stand For? For Kids
A Guide to Building Character
by Barbara A. Lewis
True stories, inspiring quotations, thought-provoking dilemmas, and activities help elementary school children build positive character traits including caring, fairness, respect, and responsibility. From the best-selling author of *What Do You Stand For? For Teens.* Includes updated resources. For ages 7–12.
$14.95; 176 pp.; softcover; B&W photos and illus.; 7¼" x 9"

The Bully Free Classroom™
Over 100 Tips and Strategies for Teachers K–8
by Allan L. Beane, Ph.D.
Positive and practical, this solution-filled book can make any classroom a place where all students are free to learn without fear. It spells out 100 proven strategies teachers can start using immediately. Includes true stories, checklists, resources, and reproducible handout masters. For teachers, grades K–8. *$24.95; 176 pp.; softcover; 8½" x 11"*

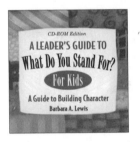

A Leader's Guide to What Do You Stand For? For Kids CD-ROM
Eleven easy-to-use lessons reinforce and expand the messages of the student book. Includes additional dilemmas and reproducibles. For teachers, grades 1–6.
$19.95; Macintosh and PC compatible, 5" CD-ROM, reproducible handout masters.

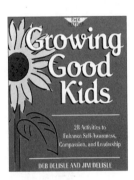

Growing Good Kids
28 Activities to Enhance Self-Awareness, Compassion, and Leadership
by Deb Delisle and Jim Delisle, Ph.D.
Created by teachers and classroom-tested, these fun and meaningful enrichment activities build children's skills in problem solving, decision making, cooperative learning, divergent thinking, and communication. For grades 3–8. *$21.95; 168 pp.; softcover; illus.; 8½" x 11"*

Stick Up for Yourself!
Every Kid's Guide to Personal Power and Positive Self-Esteem
Revised and Updated
by Gershen Kaufman, Ph.D., Lev Raphael, Ph.D., and Pamela Espeland
Simple text teaches assertiveness, responsibility, relationship skills, choice making, problem solving, and goal setting.
For ages 8–12. *$11.95; 128 pp.; softcover; illus.; 6" x 9"*

Teacher's Guide
A 10-Part Course in Self-Esteem and Assertiveness for Kids
Revised and Updated
For teachers, grades 3–7. *$21.95; 128 pp.; softcover; 8½" x 11"*

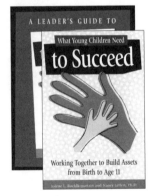

What Young Children Need to Succeed
Working Together to Build Assets from Birth to Age 11
by Jolene L. Roehlkepartain and Nancy Leffert, Ph.D.
Based on groundbreaking research, this book helps adults create a firm foundation for children from day one. For parents, teachers, all other caring adults, and children. *$11.95; 320 pp.; softcover; illus.; 5¼" x 8"*

Leader's Guide
For educators, preschool through grade 6.
$19.95; 152 pp.; softcover; 8½" x 10⅞"

To place an order or to request a free catalog of SELF-HELP FOR KIDS® and SELF-HELP FOR TEENS® materials, please write, call, email, or visit our Web site:

Free Spirit Publishing Inc.
217 Fifth Avenue North • Suite 200 • Minneapolis, MN 55401-1299
toll-free 800.735.7323 • local 612.338.2068 • fax 612.337.5050
help4kids@freespirit.com • www.freespirit.com